AF262704

TESTIMONIALS

"This book is a survival manual for the modern scholar. It is a must-read for any student who wants to be Dr. FAMOUS without losing their mind. Dr Gladys offers real-world 'hacks' for staying productive and avoiding the ABD trap."

Dr. Umut Aslan,
President Growth and Success Institute

"This book is the best friend one can have for the lonely trek into the desert of writing a dissertation. Dr. Ann provides a steady and reassuring hand and voice that makes the challenging and difficult realities of writing a dissertation into a palpable dream that "you can do this." The book makes the arduous, seemingly unsurmountable, and arid dissertation path into one that's encouraging to keep going while maintaining a sane mind and your relationships intact. The book guides you to avoid the hazards and distractions and provides tips, tricks, and strategies to reach your goal—a completed dissertation. Written in an engaging and uplifting manner, it relieves the anxieties in writing a dissertation from start to finish."

Dr. Regina Flores-Tercero,
Author, Business Consultant, Finance Executive,
Distinguished Toastmaster

"The Sane Dissertation is the book I truly needed at the beginning of my doctoral journey. With her trademark clarity, compassion, and hard-earned wisdom, Dr. Ann Gladys demystifies the dissertation process while speaking directly to the emotional realities—imposter syndrome, isolation, and overwhelm—that affected my progress. With her steady guidance and unwavering support, I completed my dissertation. Now you can learn from her, too."

**Dr. Betsy Henderson,
M.A., LCMFT, LMFT, LCAC, SHRM-CP,
Owner & Therapist, Metamorphosis Center LLC**

"As one of Dr. Ann Gladys's dissertation students, I had the rare privilege of experiencing firsthand the wisdom, the compassion, and the steady guidance that she pours into *The Sane Dissertation*. Dr. Gladys didn't just help me to complete a manuscript — she helped me to navigate the emotional, the intellectual, and the very human journey to the completion of my dissertation. She gives her students tough love. Her ability to blend structure with encouragement, and high standards with genuine empathy, made all the difference during the moments when doubt, fatigue, or "life happens" situations, threatened to derail my progress. This book captures her voice exactly as I remember it: clear, practical, motivating, and deeply invested in the success of her students. If you are embarking on the dissertation path, consider using this book like a trusted mentor at your side. It is a reflection of the extraordinary educator who guided me all the way to the dissertation finish line."

**Dr. Rick Hernandez-Gist, BA, MA, MFA, PhD
Performing Artist, Director, Producer, Arts Administrator**

"Dr. Ann Gladys is truly an expert on the dissertation process she writes about. Having served on my dissertation committee and as a Professor for my class, I know she provides amazing, specific feedback on each dissertation to help get it done well and efficiently. Now she is able to take her collective knowledge and wisdom from her academic career and provide general guidance to all of her lucky readers to help them become "Dr. Famous"."

Dr. Matthew Hudson,
Contracts Manager, Business Leadership Academic

"This book is a gift for Doctoral candidates. As one of the fortunate individuals who had Dr. Gladys on my dissertation committee, I can say with certainty that without her gentle reminders echoing in my mind, I might not have the "Dr." in front of my name today. If you are currently in the dissertation process or even contemplating a doctoral program, I highly recommend keeping this book nearby. It serves as a warm, encouraging, and optimistic—yet realistic—companion. This guide will go a long way in keeping you "sane" as you progress through this remarkable journey (and you will!)."

Dr. Randy Kasper
Manager, School for Imagery and Health,
Speaker, Psychotherapist, Professor

"Dr. Gladys has done it again with a fantastic, practical, and highly digestible publication that truly delivers. Her emphasis on staying laser-focused on the dissertation, minimizing distractions, and committing fully to the process, has proven to be incredibly effective. She reminds students that while the dissertation is only one part of the journey, success comes from taking it one focused bite at a time."

Dr. Shenica S. Nelson,
Author and Work-Life Balance Researcher,
Strategic Business Advisor

"Dr. Gladys's book offers the kind of insightful, compassionate guidance that helps you navigate the dissertation process with clarity, confidence, and your wellbeing intact. In her book, Dr. Gladys provides practical strategies that make the work feel manageable and far less isolating, from planning and writing to staying motivated through setbacks. Her voice reflects why she is one of the most caring and effective chairs, with high standards paired with steady encouragement that helps you finish strong without losing what matters most."

Dr. Ali Nikbakht,
Executive Clinical Director, We Level Up California

"In this book, Ann shares practical steps for breaking down the dissertation process and building an effective timeline. As my dissertation chair, Dr. Ann Gladys was a supportive mentor who guided me through tough challenges. This book serves as an essential guide to achieving dissertation success. If you don't have Ann as a mentor, this book is the next best thing."

Dr. Tim Ratliff Sr. CWO3 USN (ret)

"*The Sane Dissertation: Writing Your Dissertation without Losing Your Family, Your Friends, and Your Mind!* is an excellent resource that captures the real challenges doctoral students face, including imposter syndrome, procrastination, and distraction. Dr. Gladys's mentorship, guidance, and empathy were invaluable throughout my dissertation journey, especially after I lost a loved one midway through the process. I am grateful to have earned my Doctor of Business Administration, and I give all glory to God for this accomplishment."

Dr. Bruce R. Spencer,
United States Marine Corps Combat Veteran

THE SANE DISSERTATION

Writing Your Dissertation Without Losing Your Family, Your Friends, and Your Mind!

Dr. Ann Gladys

Dissertation Progress
— Consulting & Publishing —

www.dissertationprogress.com

DEDICATION

This book is dedicated to my dissertation students: past, present, and future. For those of you for whom I have chaired your dissertations and sat on your committees, I applaud your efforts and your **results**! I have witnessed a profound growth in each of you as you endured a challenging journey from your classes through your dissertation manuscript. Along the way, I have empathized with the trials and tribulations each of you encountered. You managed to handle full-time jobs, family responsibilities, personal health issues, and a myriad of other obligations. And yet, you handled all this while ensuring that your goal of completing your dissertation remained in focus.

There were times when you felt that you could not author another word and felt like throwing your arms up in defeat! There were other times when you misplaced files and cried out in torturous pain. Through it all, however, you managed to architect brilliant dissertations, create masterful insights, and fill gaps in the research literature.

As you stay the course to "Dr. Famous," I wish you all the blessings you desire. May your next life chapter be filled with opportunities to excel and forge new academic, professional, and intellectual paths. May you use your newfound knowledge to help society. And may you know the many benefits that can accrue from your impressive achievement!

CONTENTS

Part III

Tricks of the Trade: What Your Professors Didn't Share!

Part IV

Tools of the Trade

Part V

Warnings!

Part VI

The Best Is Yet to Come!

Appendices

ACKNOWLEDGMENTS

I have written this book to bring focus to the challenges dissertation students face on the long and lonely path to completing their doctoral dissertation manuscripts. This is a path fraught with unexpected life occurrences, self-doubt, and a wide swath of trials and tribulations. In general, students are surprised to learn that authoring a dissertation is not like writing just another paper! The intense focus and organizational skills required are extraordinary. Inasmuch as universities and dissertation chairs have somewhat different requirements, this book is not meant to explain the specifics of creating a dissertation. Instead, it offers an overall description of the process, but more importantly, it addresses the seemingly insurmountable mountains doctoral candidates face and offers ideas and solutions of how to deal with them. Most past and present doctoral students will identify with the challenges, read about them and shake their heads in agreement; some of the past students will even chuckle and feel grateful the endeavor is over!

Overall, I am thankful and offer a special note of thanks to my colleagues and students who inspired me to author this book. In particular, I acknowledge and thank Dr. Brenda Wilson for her insights, expertise, and creativity. She offered amazing ideas throughout our doctoral studies at Pepperdine University, editorial support for my dissertation students, and inspiration throughout our friendship. Many thanks, Dr. Brenda!

In addition, I would also like to acknowledge some of my many students who achieved their doctorates following their dissertation work with me and served to help make this book possible. May they all continue to bask in the glory of their academic and professional accomplishments on their way to becoming "Drs. Famous!!!"

Dr. Umut Aslan
Dr. Rick Hernandez
Dr. Betsy Henderson
Dr. Matt Hudson
Dr. Randy Kasper
Dr. Brenda Mangente
Dr. Shenica Nelson
Dr. Ali Nikbakht
Dr. Tim Ratliff
Dr. Bruce Spencer
Dr. Regina Tercero

Part I

In the Beginning!

Chapter 1

A Dissertation is a Journey – But It Doesn't Need to Take Forever!

"Success is not a destination, but the road that you're on. Being successful means that you're working hard and walking your walk every day. You can only live your dream by working hard towards it. That's living your dream."

—Marlon Wayans

My experience with doctoral candidates and their dissertation experiences spans more than a decade. Aside from writing my own dissertation, I have also chaired many dissertations and have been on numerous dissertation committees. The purpose of this book is to share with you dissertation situations you may encounter and the tips, hacks, and solutions you can use to overcome the many "potholes" of the dissertation journey. This book is not the definitive guide to writing your manuscript; your university and committee will define and articulate the specifics that are necessary to comply with your institution's mandates for dissertation format and content. Rather, you can see this book as an insightful and even therapeutic guide to a process that is fraught with numerous challenges, issues, and "life happens" events. In fact, in many ways, you can use this book as *therapy* for the frustrations and difficulties you will face during the sometimes harrowing process of authoring your dissertation!

Throughout my journey and the journey of my students we experienced a wide swath of emotions from exhausting bouts of imposter syndrome to the countless "life happens" challenges (more on this in Chapter 20) that occurred during the grueling process known as creating the dissertation manuscript. For you, perhaps even more challenging than writing the dissertation, is dealing with the emotional upheaval that comes with it!

The most pervasive of these emotional trials is imposter syndrome; an internal feeling where you may see yourself as a fraud – it is where you experience extreme doubt about your capabilities even though you have been quite successful in a wide variety of endeavors. Imposter syndrome is an overpowering sense of self-doubt where you come to believe that you will be exposed as a woefully inadequate person and that any successes you have had thus far can only be attributed to sheer dumb luck! Aside from your dissertation journey, you may have experienced imposter syndrome at work, in your business, and other personal experiences. Unfortunately, it leaves you constantly worrying about meeting the expectations of others and/or feeling undeserving of your accomplishments and successes over time.

To be perfectly frank, my doctoral journey was continually colored by a fundamental belief that I wasn't even remotely capable of authoring the dissertation manuscript. Even though I achieved a 4.0 grade point average throughout my doctoral courses, writing a dissertation seemed to be an impossible dream for me.

I over-thought it to the extent that I became literally paralyzed every time I sat down to research and write! I am not sharing this with you because I want a "pity party" or that I want you to think I am a hero for having overcome my fears. I simply want to share that if you feel insecure or undeserving during your dissertation excursion, you are not alone and, more importantly, there are ways to deal with how you are feeling.

If you can identify with me, please know that your feelings are not based on reality, but instead they emanate from your own self-perception. Your first step in dealing with imposter syndrome is acknowledging it! Oftentimes this is the most difficult step because it requires you to either admit that you can't cut it or admit that you are experiencing craziness! Either way, this step is downright uncomfortable. The next step is to solicit validation from others. Basically, you want feedback that confirms that you are capable and that your fears are unfounded. The more you find your "cheerleaders" (non-doctoral colleagues) the more likely your self-perception will evolve to a more positive level. But one important thing to keep in mind is that you have already completed all your doctoral classes. This, in and of itself, should tell you that you are capable of completing the final step – your dissertation!

Please keep in mind you will invest a considerable amount of time and effort in your dissertation, to say nothing of the emotional investment! And you will likely wrestle with ongoing bouts of imposter syndrome. You will likely be faced with the guilt of not spending enough time with friends and family. And you will lose pretty much all your personal "me" time! All of this will have you questioning whether you should go on to complete this degree.

Nonetheless, as long as you remind yourself (over and over) of your personal "why" (more about this later) for this journey, your success is far more likely. It is very important that you keep reassuring yourself that what you are doing is valuable to you and to others, and that your dissertation will live on forever! After all, your research is needed because it addresses a gap in the literature and what is missing in the research of others.

With all of this in mind, it's time to look at a danger zone that will present itself to you over and over again along the way to becoming "Dr. Famous". This would be a good time to visualize the proverbial "CAUTION" sign – you know, it's the yellow tape that is placed near cliffs, on unstable walking paths, and near crime scenes! Scary, isn't it? So too, in your dissertation journey, there is yellow tape along the way. This caution sign warns you that there is one challenge that can fully derail your quest to complete your doctoral degree. The danger is clear and present, and it is the acronym "ABD". ABD translates to "All But Dissertation". Please, let me caution you that it is crucial that you do not become an "ABDer"! Being an ABDer is like wearing a scarlet letter! You will forever regret that you did not complete your dissertation, and it tells others that you lacked the tenacity, interest, diligence, and stamina to do the work! Granted, something may have gotten in the way, but other people don't know this – all they see and know is that you have not completed the work to graduate. This is probably the most disheartening place a doctoral candidate can be. While your dissertation requires focus, determination, and many actions to finish it, your job is to complete the task and graduate! The overall process of authoring your manuscript does not require that you are some kind of "brainiac," you only need to be relentless in your determination to finish!

On the Topic of Distractions

As I have emphasized to my dissertation students over and over again, when you are working on your dissertation, stay focused only on your dissertation. This means that you must minimize all distractions and be 100% laser focused. Take the time to identify and minimize those pesky distractions that hinder your productivity. This may involve turning off notifications on your phone or computer, finding a quiet workspace, or using productivity tools to block distracting websites or apps during your work sessions.

There is a price to pay for distractions! Each time you disengage from your dissertation efforts, your mind goes to another place. In doing so, you lose your train of thought and are forced to "back-pedal" – this costs you time since you need to refocus and get back into flow.

From another vantage point, do not take time off; it is not worth it! Work on your dissertation every day. If Steven King can write every day, so can you! This also applies to taking off a term or two; this will not really be a break. Instead, your dissertation will be constantly looming overhead. Ultimately, continuing to be diligent, focused, and tenacious will save you anxiety and money! However, if "life happens" and you must take a break, don't feel guilty; it's not worth it and won't help. Just get back on the horse ASAP and write something every day – even if it is just one paragraph!

Remember, everyone's productivity preferences and needs are different. Experiment with different strategies to find the ones that work best for you. It's also important to be flexible and adaptable, as circumstances may change, requiring adjustments to your prioritization and time management approach. Remember also that different time management processes work better for different individuals and situations. It's important that you experiment with various methods and then adapt them to suit your work style and your dissertation!

This brings us to very important concepts regarding procrastination, time-management, and the reality of goal achievement. At this point, I'd like to take you back to how you felt when you embarked on a new goal. Can you begin to feel that excitement of launching something new? This is the feeling of exhilaration and ambition of a new beginning – a truly clean slate! Unfortunately, this does not last, and while your goals still exist, your passion and zeal may not! Such is the case with your dissertation. When you set out on this voyage, it won't be long before you become bored and downright unhappy with the endeavor. The topic you once loved, loved, loved has become the bane of your existence! Your progress may seem almost nonexistent as you come to feel that you are actually pedaling in reverse.

So throughout your journey, it is impossible to overstate the importance of focus. This means you must do everything you can to avoid distractions. When you set to work on your dissertation, turn off your phone and notifications (yes, you can safely do this for 90 minutes). Let those you live with know that dissertation time is a "do not disturb" time (they can live without you for 90 minutes). And by all means, turn off the TV! Do whatever it takes to get into your dissertation zone. Find what gets you there: music, singing, or even meditating. If you like, you may want to have some music playing in the background. In fact, research indicates that music may help to keep you focused.[1]

All of this boils down to one thing – stay focused and keep your "eyes on the prize!"

The work to earn your doctorate is daunting. When your classes are complete, and you are all alone trying to write one of the most difficult, yet important documents of your life, it is easy to let this process go on and on and on by letting distractions get in the way! Don't let anyone or anything undermine your progress! Given the complexities of daily life, it is extraordinarily likely that you will be distracted by all-things technology. The newest tech toy can capture your attention for hours, even days! Be mindful of technology "rabbit holes." Your dissertation requires an incredible amount of intense work. But keep in mind that you only do this once – so be aware of each moment, treasure your time, and keep those bothersome distractions at bay. And remember, it's all up to you to ultimately make the choice of how to proceed and accomplish your goal of NO ABD. Oftentimes, you may feel down and that you cannot write another word. Don't have pity parties. Stay positive and maintain a real visual picture of your goal! See yourself on stage receiving your diploma. See the pride your family and friends have in you. Hear the applause as the audience cheers for you. Feel your goosebumps as you take stock of what you have accomplished!!!

Though earning a doctorate requires a substantial investment of time, effort, and dedication, the benefits are rewarding both professionally and personally. It offers you opportunities for career advancement, intellectual growth, research contributions, and recognition within your field of study. Overall, the journey of earning a doctorate is transformative. It means overcoming challenges, developing resilience, and pushing the boundaries of knowledge. During the process, you will develop your critical thinking skills and take them to a higher level; your problem-solving, time management, and project management skills will also refine themselves. These are benefits you can apply throughout your life.

But there's more! Obtaining your doctorate offers additional benefits. For example, this degree is a significant accomplishment that is widely recognized and respected. It brings prestige and recognition from your peers, colleagues, and the broader academic and professional community. A doctorate signifies a high level of academic achievement, expertise, and enhances your credibility and reputation. It is your scaffold to rewards and contributing to humanity. Such benefits are far-reaching. Having a doctorate gives you credibility. It says you are tenacious, that you are hardworking, and that you are an authority on your subject matter. And if you are interested in consulting, your dissertation can be your ticket to many high-paying consulting engagements.

One of the most gratifying accomplishments of your life will be completing your dissertation and achieving a dream. "Oh, what a feeling!" doesn't begin to describe how elated you will feel having completed this magnum opus and earned your degree! Simply keep remembering your doctorate is your dream. You have been pondering it for years, perhaps even decades before you enrolled in the degree program. This dissertation is your ticket to achieving your dream.

So, with all you have to gain, believe in yourself and make it happen! You have made it this far and you can keep going knowing that your doctorate will provide opportunities and open doors. Your job is to get up each morning, take on a superhero stance (maybe even put on a cape!), and know that you will soon achieve your goal and become Dr. Famous!

Chapter 2

WHAT IS YOUR WHY?

"The capacity to learn is a gift; the ability to learn is a skill; the willingness to learn is a choice."

—Brian Herbert

Writing a dissertation can indeed be a challenging and demanding process, requiring significant time, effort, and dedication. The personal satisfaction of completing your dissertation is deeply rooted in the intellectual growth, personal development, and sense of accomplishment it brings. It also represents a milestone in your academic or professional life that demonstrates your dedication, your expertise, and your ability to contribute to the body of knowledge.

Writing and defending your dissertation is a difficult and exacting process that literally drains your time and your intellectual energy. The act of authoring your dissertation speaks to the culmination of a long and challenging journey. But it also gives you a sense of closure and achievement, while demonstrating the successful focus of your academic endeavor.

Nonetheless, many individuals choose to go through the pain of writing a dissertation for any number of reasons. It is imperative that you know your "why." Oftentimes, when asked why they are undertaking writing a dissertation for a doctoral program, doctoral students answer, "….because it is required." But in order to actually complete the dissertation, it is important that you examine your *personal* "why."

The Why Task

Upon further examination of the "why" of your dissertation, you may simply acknowledge that it is because it is a significant academic accomplishment and it represents a culmination of your years of study and research. Or you may go deeper and state that it represents a personal challenge to develop valuable skills such as critical thinking, research methodology, data analysis, and effective communication; and that it fosters your intellectual growth, your independence as a researcher, and your deeper understanding of your chosen subject area.

The practical side of you may have a personal "why" where you want to achieve a career in academia or research-intensive fields where having a completed dissertation will enhance career prospects by demonstrating your expertise, your credibility, and your ability to do rigorous research. Knowing that your dissertation can lead to job opportunities, promotions, or research grants may easily be your personal "why!" During your dissertation writing process, you may have the chance to collaborate with colleagues, mentors, and other researchers in your field, giving you opportunities for networking professional relationships, and accessing valuable resources in the process. Your dissertation can open doors to future research projects and publishing, as well as invitations to present at conferences.

Your final manuscript can become the scaffold for further academic pursuits while contributing to future career prospects.

You may even go through the dissertation journey to please family! Perhaps your research represents a step forward in your family's academic and intellectual legacy. It may signify stature, progress, and growth within your family, as you contribute to the knowledge and understanding of a field. You may find yourself basking in a sense of pride knowing that you have contributed to your family's overall legacy of academic excellence and intellectual achievement. The completion of your dissertation is not just an individual accomplishment; it can become a success for the entire family!

Beyond familial pride, your family may provide support, encouragement, and understanding throughout the process. Celebrating the completion of a dissertation can become a joyous moment of shared success and serve as a reminder of your family's collective support and commitment to you. However, beware that while you are working on your dissertation, your family can also feel deprived of your time and attention. It is up to you to set boundaries while being reassuring and keeping your family aware of the challenges that you are facing.

Nonetheless, the more altruistic side of you may focus on the importance for you to contribute to your field through original research where you can fill in gaps in existing knowledge, and where you can propose new ideas or perspectives. Most importantly, it gives you an opportunity to make a meaningful impact on the academic community and influence future research. The process of overcoming untold challenges, conducting your research, and producing a substantial piece of scholarly insights will bring you a sense of personal fulfillment and accomplishment. After all, this is a testament to your intellect, your perseverance, and your dedication to the "why" of your goal!

I encourage you to dwell on the insights of Simon Sinek as you ponder your personal "why."[2] Sinek is a renowned author and speaker who emphasizes the significance of understanding the underlying purpose or motivation behind our actions and decisions. While he speaks to purpose and "why" in terms of organizational success, his insights have a direct bearing on our goals and personal achievements. Sinek points out that we should have three levels of approaching our intentions: the "what," the "how," and the "why," where he depicts this in terms of his Golden Circle.[3] All too often we are consumed with the "what" we are going to do. In the case of your manuscript, the overall "what" is the completion and acceptable defense of your dissertation. The "how" can take a variety of paths using the guidance documents of your university and your committee. But the tricky part comes into play with respect to the "why." Quite frequently, doctoral students either don't have, or lose sight of their personal "why" for completing the dissertation and obtaining the degree. Your "why" captures your purpose and the very reason you are taking this journey. Without it, you can easily succumb to the pressure of the process and fail to graduate.

Sinek goes on to identify exactly what your "why" adds to your life.[4] To begin with, he underscores that your "why" brings clarity to the task at hand and allows you to develop a strong focus and sense of purpose on what you are attempting to achieve. Your "why" gives you permission to address your goals and purpose by giving you guidance in your actions and decisions. Your "why" gives you an enhanced understanding of your direction and path to accomplish your goal. It is, in fact, a driving force to keep you committed and becomes the primary motivator that inspires you to conquer obstacles that cross your path during the dissertation process. It is your "why" that gives you a base camp of resilience helping you to remain focused and true to your purpose during times of fatigue and setbacks.

And if you still haven't found your "why," sheer personal satisfaction is always a go-to! The satisfaction coupled with your pursuit to explore a topic you are passionate about as you delve into the nuances of your field will give you a sense of fulfillment and joy. The process involves deep thinking, curiosity, and intellectual engagement beyond what you would expect. The bottom line is that completing your dissertation is the consummate accomplishment that brings an incredible sense of personal pride. The sense of mastery and expertise gained through this process is amazing where the process of conducting your research, analyzing the data, and writing your dissertation allows you to delve into your chosen field, giving you the opportunity to make a unique contribution to your field. The overall satisfaction of uncovering new insights, research gaps, and new knowledge is immensely gratifying.

Overall, while writing a dissertation and earning that doctorate can be an excruciating journey, the rewards and fulfillment it offers will make it a worthwhile endeavor. By discovering and embracing your "why," you will develop a deeper understanding of who you are, what your driving motivations are, and your sense of purpose. Your "why" becomes your guiding principle that defines your actions, motivates you to make a positive impact, and ultimately leads to a more fulfilling and meaningful life. All told, your passion about your field of study and your commitment to advancing knowledge in this area coupled with your personal "why" will take you on an incredible passage to becoming "Dr. Famous." If you haven't done so already, now is the time to draft your personal "why" statement for authoring your dissertation and receiving your doctorate.

In addition to your "why," you may simply be motivated by your deep passion for a general area of study. An area where you see your dissertation offering you the opportunity to explore your intellectual curiosity and contribute to the understanding of a subject. Having established your "why" and the motivation that goes with it, it is now time to address the daunting task of choosing your topic. Sounds easy, right? It is not!

Your Topic and Your Bias!

One of the most effective ways to choose a topic is to take the time to brainstorm a list of "possibles." Write down between five and ten topical areas that intrigue you and begin narrowing the field until you find the topic of your dreams. Then repeat the process by creating plausible titles that represent the topic. This process is a vital part of your journey toward becoming an expert in your field. In the course of doing this, check in with yourself to be sure that you Love, Love, Love Your Topic! In addition, when choosing your topic area, think about your future. Your dissertation is where you will be considered a "guru." So think about how this topic will launch your career path to "Dr. Famous!"

Speaking of the future, craft your title to be forward-thinking. As an example, my dissertation addressed leading remote workers. I wrote it pre-COVID, and it positioned me to be a "go-to person" in the business world of leading people you do not see, hence the title, *The Invisible Leader.*

Once you have selected a topical area, but before you begin your dissertation, read dissertations of others who have researched a similar academic area and focus on their recommendations for additional research. This can be helpful in two ways. First, it will give you a sense of how others have addressed their topics. Beginning the dissertation journey can be confusing, and you will, most likely, find yourself flailing about as you attempt to create your path forward. By canvassing the work of others, you will define your own path. Second, the recommendations for further research offered at the end of each dissertation can inspire you to delve into additional ways for sculpting and defining your topic. All too often, dissertation students try to cover an area that is far too expansive. As you define your topic, think of the general area as a forest. Then begin to limit it to a single tree in that forest, then to a branch on that tree, and finally to a leaf on the tree! While traversing this path, there are two important warnings I have for you.

Warning #1:

Do not choose a topic based on pressure from someone else! We are all influenced by others, but when it comes to your dissertation, the decision needs to be yours. Keep in mind that it is YOU who must spend what seems like countless months researching the topic; it is YOU who will need to find the participants for the research; and it is YOU who must defend the final results of the research. So choose a topic with which you have some familiarity and one YOU find absolutely fascinating!

Warning #2:

Your dissertation is not your opinion! It is meant to increase the body of knowledge based on research, both primary and secondary. A dissertation is NOT an opinion paper! Do not use personal pronouns in your dissertation, especially the word "I!" All too often, dissertation students are familiar with their topic from personal experience. And more often than not, students try to offer personal opinions that are not based on scientific research. This results in introducing personal bias, which has no place in your research and your dissertation. Overall, such bias reduces your credibility and the credibility of your dissertation. I seriously warn those of you who are pursuing a topic with which you have extensive experience, do not – I repeat, do not, fold in your personal experiential bias into your dissertation. Dissertations are about scholarly academic research, not about the trials and tribulations of your life. If you want to write about your "world," author a memoir or a "how-to" book. Again, your personal world does not belong in your dissertation manuscript! This is also an important factor to keep in mind during your proposal and final defense. When you use personal stories and personal pronouns, you create a slippery slope with your committee where your bias will become an issue and possibly put you back to square one for researching and authoring your dissertation.

In Sum

Throughout your dissertation journey, let your "why" be your north star, your impetus, and your rationale for continuous and arduous effort to scale this mountain. And as with any piece of objective writing, keep your personal biases at bay.

While the overall process of writing your dissertation requires perseverance, discipline, and critical thinking skills, it also challenges you to overcome obstacles, develop time management strategies, and refine your research and writing abilities. These techniques lead to personal growth, increased self-confidence, and an incredible sense of accomplishment.

Chapter 3

But I Feel So Alone!

*"The journey of writing a dissertation is often a solitary one,
but it is in this solitude that you discover your inner strengths
and unleash your true intellectual potential."*

— *Unknown*

Many psychologists have researched the topic of loneliness and its
effects on individuals. Among them is John C. Norcross. Norcross
is a psychologist who studied loneliness and its impact of stress and
anxiety on graduate students.[5] This can be directly related to the
experience of loneliness during the dissertation process. Another
noteworthy researcher on the topic is John T. Cacioppo, who
extensively studied loneliness and its effects on physical and mental
health. His work included numerous studies on the psychological
and physiological impacts of social isolation.[6] In addition, Juli-
anne Holt-Lunstad researched the impact of loneliness and the
consequences to social relationships.[7] More specifically, her work
highlighted the adverse effects of social isolation and loneliness
on physical health, including the increased risk of cardiovascular
disease and mortality. These psychologists offer insights into
loneliness and have helped shed light on the detrimental effects
of prolonged loneliness.

Loneliness and frustration are among the most common emotions experienced by many doctoral students throughout their academic course journey. But the process of completing a dissertation can be even more challenging and demanding than the coursework, requiring long hours of solitary work and intense focus. In this chapter, I will explore the loneliness and frustration felt by dissertation students and discuss the causes and potential strategies to cope with these emotions.

Your dissertation journey can be very isolating since no one else is working on the same project that you are researching. Your topic is constantly on your mind, and quite frankly, most people don't understand it and really don't want to hear about it! This results in you and them keeping a distance from one another.

According to a report by the U.S. Surgeon General Dr. Vivek Murthy, loneliness is as deadly as smoking 15 cigarettes a day! Though loneliness and isolation became a hot topic during the pandemic, it was a problematic issue even before 2020. According to the Surgeon General's report, loneliness causes inflammation, increases blood pressure, and elevates stress hormones.[8]

But don't despair, you can mitigate these issues with short spurts of exercise, a very brief call to someone you haven't chatted with in some time, or even by striking up a conversation with someone in line in a coffee shop! So be sure to make at least one human connection every day of your dissertation journey.[9]

Please keep in mind that you are not alone in your loneliness! It is a common feeling among dissertation students, mainly due to the independent nature of the task. Unlike traditional classroom settings that you have become used to over the last several years, where you and your fellow students engage in regular interactions with each other and your professors, your dissertation research involves long hours knee-deep in peer-reviewed journal articles, books, laboratories, or at home alongside your computer while you are creating your literature review, collecting data, and performing analyses. This isolation can create a sense of disconnect, as you miss social support and face-to-face interaction.

In addition, the pressure to meet your milestones and produce high-quality work will only intensify your feelings of loneliness. You will often experience the self-imposed isolation necessary to maintain your sense of focus and concentrate solely on your research. Ultimately, this will lead you to a sense of disconnect from your former social circles and a deep feeling of loss of connection with friends, family, and the broader academic community. Unfortunately, many, if not all of your friends, have no clue about what it is like to write a dissertation. You must accept the fact that this forces you to talk about something other than your dissertation – which is good since your dissertation is already consuming most of your life! We all agree that friends are important, BUT some will not understand your situation and will temporarily or permanently disappear. You may even get to thinking that some of them are jealous and want to sabotage your work. You must keep in mind that you are only one document away from being called "doctor!" The bottom line is that while jealousy sounds silly, some of your "friends" will feel differently about you. Don't keep these negative personalities in your circle of friends – at least not until you have finished your dissertation. In the grand scheme of things, if you have one or more of these friends, dump them – these people are probably not your real friends!

Furthermore, the mere nature of research can contribute to frustration since the process involves numerous challenges, such as encountering unforeseen obstacles, struggling to collect and analyze data, grappling with complex theories and concepts, and facing setbacks or revisions. These difficulties can evoke heightened feelings of frustration, as you may question your abilities, become overwhelmed by the magnitude of the task, or feel stuck in a cycle of trial and error.

Moreover, the long duration of the dissertation process, which will most likely span years, can further compound feelings of frustration. Undoubtedly, your journey will involve facing multiple revisions, setbacks, and uncertainties, which can test both your patience and your resilience. This prolonged period of uncertainty and hard work can leave you feeling discouraged and questioning your progress and your resolve, ultimately impacting your success.

To cope with the loneliness and frustration experienced during the dissertation process, there are several strategies you can employ. First and foremost, find yourself a strong support network – this is absolutely essential. Working with peers, mentors, or support groups can give you emotional support, validation, and a sense of camaraderie. Participating in regular discussions, sharing experiences, and seeking advice from those who have gone through similar challenges can help alleviate feelings of isolation and provide valuable insights and encouragement. Believe me, it is so reassuring to hear someone say, "I understand what you are going through – take it one step at a time – and never give up! I believe in you!"

Additionally, setting realistic expectations and establishing a well-defined schedule can help create a sense of calm for you. Perhaps the single most important protocol you can activate is breaking down the dissertation process into manageable tasks. This means identifying tasks that are right sized for you. For some students, a manageable task is writing a literature review. However, for most students, this task is seen as overwhelming! Consider a task that is "just right" for you (remember Goldilocks?) This may be finding and reading just one or two peer-reviewed journal articles this week on your topic area. Setting achievable goals can create a sense of progress and accomplishment, while reducing that awful sense of being overwhelmed. Celebrating milestones along the way can also provide you with motivation and reinforce your belief in your ability to complete the dissertation successfully.

Your effective time management while practicing self-care is crucial for managing and mitigating the effects of loneliness and frustration. Prioritizing short-regular breaks, maintaining a healthy work-life balance, and engaging in activities aside from research can help reduce your stress and prevent burnout. It is important that you acknowledge and keep in mind that you are physically vulnerable under this high-stress process. So be sure to take care of #1 – YOU!

Finding some activities that serve as "break time" will certainly help. Engaging in a hobby, exercising, socializing, or seeking support from a therapist or counselor can contribute to your overall well-being and combat those dreaded feelings of loneliness and isolation. In addition, guidance from mentors and advisors can provide clarity and support during your dissertation journey, thereby reducing loneliness and providing support for your manuscript. Regular meetings with your dissertation chair can offer valuable feedback, guidance, and perspective. Please note that dissertation chairs have crowded schedules, requiring you to be extremely flexible! It is important you initiate and maintain open communication with your chair about your feelings of loneliness and frustration. Doing this will encourage your chair to provide tailored support and strategies to help reduce the feelings of overwhelm and isolation during your dissertation journey. As a side note, one issue that has been known to occur is that sometimes when a chair offers guidance, the student ignores the guidance! Never, never, never ignore your chair's guidance!!!

Lastly, by cultivating a positive mentality and reframing challenges as learning opportunities, you can transform feelings of isolation into a growth mindset. Embracing a growth mindset, acknowledging setbacks as part of the learning process, and celebrating even the small victories can foster resilience and a sense of progress. Engaging in these activities throughout your dissertation journey can help you create and maintain a positive way of thinking and reduce moments of frustration.

Part II

THE PIECES AND PARTS!

Chapter 4

YOUR ABSTRACT IS YOUR HOOK!

"As long as it's something that makes readers think, 'I want to know more about this' the hook has done its job."
— *Savannah Gilbo*

Your abstract is what captures your reader to read on – it is your hook. Though your abstract should be the last thing you write in your dissertation manuscript, you will most likely be tempted to write it early on and then go back and revise it after you have completed your research. Unfortunately, the abstract can be very difficult to author; you must succinctly tell the world about your 30,000 + word dissertation in 250-500 words or less! And even more intimidating is that these are the words that will either engage or disengage your reader. They are the words that will make the difference whether your dissertation is read or not! The importance of your abstract is that it must be a strong hook in capturing the attention of your potential readers and drawing them into a study that differentiates your work from yet another dull and boring treatise. Your job in the abstract is to make your dissertation downright enticing! A well-crafted hook in your abstract has the power to intrigue, captivate, and engage readers from the very beginning while setting the stage for a memorable reading experience. This means that you avoid technical and otherwise dry language and communicate in a manner that is understandable to a broad audience.

The ingredients of your dissertation abstract include the following brief statements: your purpose, research question(s), research methodology and data collection, and your overall high-level key findings. As you author your abstract, use the past tense since the abstract describes what has already been researched.

Please note, the abstract should be straightforward, concise, engaging, and directly related to your research without necessitating citations. It should capture the reader's attention and motivate them to continue reading the rest of your dissertation. Keep in mind that your abstract is the first thing readers read about your research, so remember that first impressions count!

As always, it is important to consider the guidelines and expectations of your discipline, institution, and chair. Consult with your dissertation chair or refer to dissertation writing resources in your field for additional guidance on creating an effective hook for your abstract. As a side note, don't be disappointed if only sparse guidance exists for writing an abstract since very few researchers are able to write a good one!

Chapter 5

CONTINUE TO ENGAGE YOUR READER IN YOUR FIRST DISSERTATION CHAPTER

"Chapter 1 [of the dissertation] serves as the bridge between the existing body of knowledge and the researcher's study, providing a comprehensive review of relevant literature and theoretical frameworks. It lays the groundwork for the research by demonstrating the gaps and opportunities that the study aims to address."

— R. Murray Thomas

In addition to your abstract, your first chapter must be engaging, well-written, focused, and succinct. It too must hook the reader. It must be well-researched. And in conjunction with your purpose statement, it must articulate a sound and convincing argument. Writing this first chapter of your dissertation, commonly known as the Introduction Chapter, is critical since it sets the stage for your research and provides a context for the study. In the initial paragraphs of this chapter, you might share a surprising or intriguing fact/statistic, or you can use a quotation that is impactful and directly related to your research.

As you begin to understand, and I mean thoroughly understand, the *purpose* of your dissertation, it will be on your mind virtually every day and night! Your well-articulated purpose provides the reader with a firm idea of the "why" of your dissertation. It also provides you with a reflection point to refer to throughout your dissertation journey in order to keep you from going down the proverbial rabbit holes and losing direction – your purpose will keep you on point! All too often, dissertation students think of new topics for research while authoring their manuscript. This frequently results in many hours of researching the wrong subject! Though these new ideas are interesting, and you certainly don't want them to be forgotten, just annotate them in a "parking lot." That is to say, place them in a list for safekeeping for future (post-doctorate) research.

One of the more interesting ways to begin authoring Chapter 1 is with an interesting statistic about your intended subject matter. This can capture the reader's attention, create a sense of curiosity, and motivate them to continue reading. For example, if your dissertation addresses illiteracy, you might include the following, "Research shows that X% of the population in the United States is illiterate and that this group tends to commit a disproportionate percentage of all crimes." Now you have your readers wondering about the ill effects of illiteracy, the current ways society is addressing the issue, and how they can become a part of the solution.

Be sure to include a clear and succinct introduction. Offer readers an insight into the origins of the topic, where there may be disconnects between the probable and current solutions. Introduce your topic and provide background information. Then state the research problem you intend to address and study, as well as the research questions that comprise the focus of your dissertation.

Now is the time to articulate the significance of your study. This is where you communicate why your research is important to the field of study and relevant for the future. It is critical that you express that your work will study something different than prior research by writing about the gaps in the existing literature and the practical implications of your research. Don't be afraid to get into "the good, the bad, and the ugly" of your topic. Offer insights into where your field of study has offered benefits in the past, what lessons were learned, and what went so wrong that new insights and processes are absolutely required.

Along with the significance of the study, it is important to consider and articulate the ethical factors of your research, and how it will benefit and not harm members of society. This is where you explain how you emphasize your personal ethical conduct throughout your study. For example, how will you contain and mitigate your personal bias through your personal ethos? The overall process includes a discussion of the ethics of your research, such as informed consent, confidentiality, and data protection. These are areas you will include in your application to the IRB (more about this in the chapter regarding methodology). While you will elaborate on the ethics side of your research in Chapter 3 of your dissertation, Chapter 1 is where you communicate to the reader that you are aware of potential ethical issues associated with your study.

In Chapter 1, you provide initial clarity regarding informed consent wherein you describe the manner in which you will ensure that participants in your research have been informed about the topic, how you are conducting the research with participants, and that they have the right to opt out the research at any point in the interview or survey. As it relates to confidentiality in qualitative research, you will explain to your participants that their individual responses to your questions will not disclose their identity. You will also share the manner in which you intend to protect participant identity in your findings. Again, in Chapter 1, you will elaborate at a very high level, the design and methodology (qualitative, quantitative, mixed methods).

At the conclusion of Chapter 1, you will offer an overview of your dissertation structure. This is where you outline and summarize the organization and architecture of your dissertation. Be sure to articulate the main chapters of your manuscript, their overall content, and how they will address the research problem and the associated objectives of your dissertation. Be sure to offer a summary of the main points in Chapter 1, along with a clear transition to Chapter 2 of the dissertation. Most importantly, emphasize again the significance of your research and its potential contribution to your field of study.

All told, your Chapter 1 should be 15 to 20 pages in length. Be sure to keep the chapter concise and focused, avoiding excessive background information, hyperbole, or tangents/rabbit holes! Simultaneously, keep in mind that the structure and requirements of this first chapter (see Appendix A for Chapter Contents for Each of the Dissertation Chapters) may vary depending on your topic, your chair, your discipline, and the guidelines provided by your institution. It is your job to consult with your chair and refer to your university dissertation writing resources that are specific to your field.

Chapter 6

YOUR LIT REVIEW, IT'S LIKE GOING FISHING!

"A literature review is not a mere summary of existing research; it is a critical engagement with the ideas and methodologies that have shaped the field. It requires us to analyze, synthesize, and evaluate the scholarly conversations, ultimately positioning our own work within this complex web of knowledge."

— John Creswell

Interestingly, one of the first questions doctoral students ask is, "How long does my Literature Review need to be?" The answer is, "that depends!" In general, you can expect your lit review to be about 40 pages. But the real answer comes down to your topic and the gap between current research and the focus of your study. The lit review is Chapter 2 of your dissertation, and, in my humble opinion, it is the most grueling of the chapters! This is where you keep searching for information about your topic and articulating where the gaps exist in the current research with respect to your specific topic.

In part, the reason the lit review is so grueling is that it requires you to critically analyze and synthesize an inordinate amount of peer-reviewed research and publications related to your specific topic.

In order to remain on track, each time you begin to work on your lit review, reread and contemplate your topic. This may sound a bit bizarre, but all too often students go off on tangents and end up investing a significant amount of time on research unrelated or only marginally related to their topic! So keep rereading your dissertation title! Also keep in mind that a clearly defined scope and focus of your literature review will ensure that your research time is well spent.

As you continue to create your lit review, continually reevaluate the credibility, the value, and the overall quality of the sources you find. Research the expertise of the authors you cite, as well as the publication's reputation. Strength in these areas is incredibly important to underscore the credibility of your dissertation. Stay away from blogs, newsletters, pop culture magazines, and Wikipedia as sources for your lit review. You will also need to be careful with any information you receive via artificial intelligence (AI) platforms. Be sure to "reverse engineer" information from AI platforms to find citations and references in order to double-check the accuracy of the information.

So, now that you are ready to jump head-first into the ocean of relevant research on your topic, create a process for organizing and finding common patterns in the literature, as well as gaps that deserve additional exploration. As you set to organize the research, use some form of software such as Excel so that you can slice and dice information as needed. For example, if you are researching several different employee areas such as engagement, retention, training, etc. you can sort your references by topic. Or if you are looking for all the references by a given author such as Adam Grant, you can sort your spreadsheet so that his works are grouped and easily accessed. This organizational framework can use architectures such as thematic, researcher, chronological, theoretical, statistical, etc. When you group your literature based on similarities or differences, it will help you identify the main themes or arguments that emerge from the literature.

When it comes time to synthesize your information, you can begin by examining the strengths or weaknesses of the research contained in the individual pieces of literature. This is where you can scrutinize any conflicting findings and evaluate the implications of the research. The diligent work you do in your lit review will pay off in terms of helping you identify the limitations and/or gaps in the literature. After all, if research has already covered what you intend to study, then there is no need to pursue a topic that has already been addressed! As you find gaps in the literature, you can identify where your research will make a vital and unique contribution. This process allows you to begin to further articulate your research questions or hypotheses.

The construct of your lit review begins with an introduction that gives the reader the context and a firm idea of the objective of your work. It's a good idea to create an outline of possible section headers to help guide you in the review of the literature. Your section headers can include the themes, concepts, and theories you plan to explore.

As you delve into specific journal articles and books, pay particular attention to the contributions, limitations, and the implications of each piece of research. Note also the references used by each author. These references can lead you to additional studies that can help build your lit review. The process of using references from journal articles is a process I like to call "going fishing" since each article contains additional sources of information for your lit review!

Please keep in mind that it is very easy to fall into a rabbit hole as you work on your lit review. Oftentimes, my students will say, "but the article looked soooo interesting" even though it wasn't even remotely related to their topic! Therefore, during each step of your lit review process, keep asking yourself if this piece of literature is actually germane to your research.

While you may be tempted to revise and edit your lit review chapter while you are in the midst of authoring your first draft, DON'T! If you do this, it will drag you into the abyss of never finishing the chapter. Worse yet, if you constantly revise and edit the other chapters as well, you will remain ABD – All But Dissertation! Obviously, there is a time for revisions, but it is after you have completed the first draft.

Through your work on this and other chapters, make absolutely sure that you properly cite all the sources you have used. Oftentimes, doctoral students say they already knew something they wrote and therefore did not need to offer a citation. Keep in mind that your dissertation is not about you or what you already know – it is about researching and finding *authoritative* sources and information that has been acquired through the significant research of others. Please know that the more you cite, the better you look! One easy way to ensure that you are citing appropriately is to find the source of any statistic you use. Another way is to read each sentence you have written and ask yourself, "says who?" Remember, it is your responsibility to maintain academic integrity by appropriately citing and referencing all the sources you have used. All told, peer-reviewed journal articles are the staff of life for your dissertation – be constantly on the lookout for the next piece of research that will enhance your dissertation.

METHODOLOGY – YOUR PLAN OF ATTACK!

"Planning is bringing the future into the present so that you can do something about it now."

— *Alan Lakein*

As I approached this chapter, I was reminded of a dissertation student of mine who had mapped out her methodology plan for conducting her research well in advance of defending her proposal. She had decided on performing quantitative research and had done the advance planning for surveying a specific organization in the military. Her point of contact in the military complex committed to sending the survey throughout the organization after the dissertation proposal received approval from the IRB. Unfortunately, when the time came to send out the survey, the point of contact declared that he did not have the right to send the survey and the legal department declined the request to engage the organization. As a result, the dissertation student was left to send the survey through other means, costing her considerable time and frustration!

Chapter 3 of a dissertation typically focuses on the research methodology employed to conduct the study. It outlines the specific methods, procedures, and approaches used to gather and analyze data, as well as the overall research design (Appendix B). The methodology chapter is crucial because it provides a clear understanding of how you will conduct your research and defines the validity and reliability of the findings you accrue in the process of conducting and analyzing your research.

Your plan of attack for your dissertation is the method you are going to use to do the research that addresses the formal research questions you establish. There are primarily three approaches: quantitative (i.e. statistical), qualitative (robust interviews and fact gathering), and a mixed methods approach that combines quantitative and qualitative.

Your dissertation is an analysis that weaves together your research of the current body of knowledge along with your individual research (quantitative, qualitative, or mixed methods). The synthesis of your literature research and your participant research combines to create a dissertation that adds to the existing body of knowledge. Quantitative research is the fastest route to completing the research for your dissertation, but not necessarily the best. Qualitative research is time-intensive but offers more robust insights into the opinions of your participant pool, allowing you to perform a thematic analysis by identifying the categories and themes that dominate the participant interviews.

The following components typically comprise the dissertation methodology chapter and include a description of your research design, a definition of your selection process for participants including recruitment, an explanation of your data collection process, a characterization of your data analysis, a definition of your approach to establishing validity and reliability, and a complete discussion of the ethical considerations employed by your research. The paragraphs below offer additional elaboration on these dissertation areas.

Your Target Population and Sampling Plan

You will generally begin your Chapter 3 with an introduction that reestablishes your purpose and articulates your research question(s) and/or hypotheses. It is therefore important that you identify your target population along with your sample criteria.

When selecting your study participants, one of the most interesting and thought-provoking actions you will take in your research is deciding who should participate in your study. Overall, this process includes details about the target population, the sampling technique used, sample size considerations, and any specific criteria for inclusion or exclusion. One aspect of participant selection is that of filtering. All too often, doctoral students fail to consider exactly what subset/sample of a population is right for their study. For the process of participant selection, you will first need to define the population. For example, are you interested in a population of Millennial employees? In order to filter your population, you may want to only consider Millennials working in the Information Technology industry. You might also want to filter your population by a specific geographic area, such as Southern California. Additionally, depending on your topic, you can further filter by single Millennials.

As an example, consider the following.

The target population for this study is information technology (IT) managers of federal contracts in the San Diego Area. The criteria for selection of the sample of participants is that each participant is a manager, is employed in San Diego by a firm that supports federal IT contracts and has been employed for at least the last five years by a federal IT contractor. Participants will be drawn from the National Defense Industrial Association (NDIA) professional association in Southern California whose membership is comprised primarily of companies that hold federal IT contracts. This approach is consistent with guidance as it relates to sample selection and procedures.[10]

Your sampling plan addresses the methodology you will use for obtaining participants for your qualitative research. Below is an example of a sampling plan for qualitative research. The plan articulates the filters that are considered in the sampling process.

Through purposeful sampling via coordination with the chairperson of the NDIA Chapter in San Diego, an invitation will be sent to the general membership to recruit participants by using questions that address position (managerial), tenure (at least five years), and corporate affiliation (a firm that supports federal IT contracts). The invitation will include a statement that indicates: that participation is voluntary; the results of the research and future participation in a study will be confidential; the stipulation that the respondent willingly agrees to participate in the study; and that the survey results will be used to increase the body of knowledge concerning effective leadership. Drawing from responses that meet the criteria of this study, 12 participants will be invited to participate on a "first received" basis. That is to say, the first 12 responses that fulfill the sampling criteria will be selected to participate in the study. Following their selection, potential participants will be contacted by phone to establish rapport, ensure each participant meets the criteria for participation in the study, and to review the process, parameters, and purpose of the study. Accordingly, sampling procedures that are well-defined serve to provide for and enhance the credibility of the study.[11]

As you architect your sampling plan, keep in mind that your research must be conducted in accordance with IRB considerations for respect for human subjects. Overall, guidance and research procedures include the following elements you will disclose to your participants: description and purpose of your study; the logistics of the interview itself; latitude for voluntary participation and option to withdrawal; confidentiality; point of contact information; opportunity to review transcripts; and signatory blocks.[12]

It is important to note that research ethics are absolutely critical. In your dissertation proposal, you must speak to ethical considerations and measures you will take to protect your participants' rights and maintain their anonymity (for statistical surveys) and confidentiality (for qualitative interviews). As part of this process, addressing informed consent, privacy, ethical guidelines, and Institutional Review Board requirements are integral in this area of ethical consideration.

Your interface with your study participants must be based on their voluntary participation and consent. Additionally, your participants must be informed of their right to withdraw from the study at any time with no repercussions; that their names will be coded to protect their identities so they will have anonymity in your dissertation manuscript; and that the data associated with their interviews will be redacted to protect their identity. It is important that you be open with the participants as it relates to fully describing interview participation and the recording thereof.[13]

Further reducing risk to your participants is your procedure for data protection and confidentiality by way of encrypted electronic files and safe-secured recordings. Prior to and during the interviews, assure your participants of the confidentiality of the security processes associated with their interviews.

In your research design, you will describe and explain the overall approach and design of the study, such as quantitative, qualitative, or mixed methods. In this section, you will justify the design and offer your reasoning that the approach is appropriate for addressing the research questions as well as the research objectives.

Data Collection

Once you have selected and defined your sample of participants, you will turn your attention toward creating data collection procedures. This is the time to outline the methods and instruments you will use to collect data. In order to do this, you will need to create a detailed description of the data collection techniques, such as: the survey instrument(s) you intend to use if you plan to employ a quantitative approach in your dissertation; the construct of participant interviews (i.e. interview questions) if your plan includes a qualitative approach; and any qualitative observation or experimental techniques you plan to use. When defining the data collection procedures, be sure to explain in very detailed and explicit terms how data will be gathered, including the time frame, location, and any ethical considerations or permissions you plan to obtain.

Quantitative Approach

If you choose a quantitative approach for your research, you will outline the statistical technique(s) you will employ to analyze the data you collect. This may include descriptive statistics (e.g., mean, bar charts, percentages, etc.), inferential statistics (e.g., t-tests, ANOVA, regression analysis, etc.), or other advanced statistical methods. It is important to justify the selection of specific analyses and explain how each addresses your hypotheses.

Integral to the quantitative approach is the requirement to ensure your survey is both valid and reliable. Simply put, you can't just dream up some questions and hope your study has credibility! This means conducting a pilot test of the survey you designed or using a survey instrument that has already been found to be both valid and reliable. Regardless of the route you take, it is incumbent upon you to describe and ensure the validity and reliability of the measurement instrument, control extraneous variables, and address potential sources of bias.

Qualitative Approach

A qualitative dissertation methodology is a research approach that focuses on understanding and interpreting subjective experiences, meanings, and social phenomena. It involves collecting and analyzing verbal responses that can generate robust descriptions of your research topic. The purpose of qualitative research is to examine complex phenomena with an in-depth understanding using methods such as interviews, observations, and textual analysis.

The Interview Process

Your qualitative interviews should be conducted in a neutral setting, in person, via video, or telephonically. A best practice with regard to conducting interviews is that you use the same medium for all interviews. That is to say, if you perform in-person interviews, then all your interviews should be in-person. The same holds true for telephonic and video interviews. Choose one method that works for all participants and use it throughout.

The interviews should be semi-structured with open-ended questions that allow for follow-up questions. Your data may be collected via video to afford you an insight into the body language of your participants. In addition, you will transcribe the verbal portion of the interview. The subsequent review process of the interviews should include a textual analysis of the interview as well as the interview transcript. Following each interview, be sure to safely store the digital interviews. Similarly, as you transcribe each interview, generate a transcript and store it as an electronically encrypted file. Access to your interviews will be controlled by you, and it is your responsibility to ensure the safety and privacy of your participants' interviews.

In general, each interview should last about 30 minutes. If you plan for longer interviews, you may lose those potential participants who are not willing to share an hour or more of their time. Note: prior to and during the interviews, you will need to request consent for recording the session. You must also inform your participants of their right to withdraw from the interview at any time with no repercussions to them. Following the interview and transcription process, you may, at your discretion, send the transcript to the individual participant for them to review for accuracy. Keep in mind that this step is not a requirement in general, and if you choose to send transcripts to your participants, you will lengthen the overall interview process to time-consuming and possibly iterative reviews!

So, how do you know that you have interviewed enough participants? This is the point at which you consider the interview process complete, and it is when you reach what is known as data saturation. The process of data saturation (i.e. receiving the same answers multiple times to the interview questions from your participants) is the driving force for knowing when you have performed a sufficient number of interviews. There are two additional requirements for you to consider when interviewing. The first is validity, and the second is reliability.

Validity. The strategy for ensuring the validity of your study includes the review, coding, and thematic analysis of the interview data; and should be conducted by you as well as a peer reviewer. The use of a peer reviewer to code and analyze the data provides inter-rater reliability to support the validity of the study. [14] In this process, you will compare the results of an independent reviewer and where differences exist in coding, discussion will ensue until discrepancies are resolved and consensus is achieved. This approach is designed to support the internal validity of the study and for bracketing bias that might influence conclusions.[15] The validity of the study is also strengthened by a review of each participant of his/her interview transcript. Creswell offers guidance in this regard by stating, "…it [validity] is based on determining whether the findings are accurate from the standpoint of the researcher, the participant, or other readers of an account…".[16] Overall, the validity of the analysis and interpretations of this study are supported by the process, intercoder-reliability, and participant review of the transcript.

Reliability. In terms of reliability, the process of your study must lend itself to repeatable and consistent results. The first step is a random selection process to engage participants. The operative word here is "random." The next step consists of recording and transcribing the interviews. The final step is inter-rater analysis and consensus. Once again, this is where you engage a person knowledgeable in qualitative research and familiar with your dissertation topic.

Managing Your Interview Scripts

Now is the time for you to roll up your sleeves for the hard work of analyzing the information you received from your participants' interviews. Overall, the qualitative approach to research involves coding, thematic analysis, content analysis, or other interpretive techniques. This means that you will need to describe how you managed the information you gathered, the manner in which you organized the information, and how you interpreted the responses to the interview questions with the purpose of finding patterns, themes, and relationships.

Unless you are somewhat of a masochist and are ready for an inordinate amount of work in managing the interview information from your participants (this could easily be several hundred pages!), you will want to use software designed for transcribing and coding your participant interviews. The identification and discussion of the software for this process will be included in your methodology chapter. There are a number of software packages you can employ for transcription and categorization of your interview responses. Among these are HyperRESEARCH, HyperTRANSCRIBE, Zoom Transcribe, Delve, etc.

Identifying Your Themes

But there's more – this is not a solo show! The qualitative process also includes intercoder reliability. Intercoder reliability is achieved when there is consensus between you and your peer reviewer. This is the agreement you and your peer reviewer have achieved based on the patterns, themes, and relationships each of you has identified while reviewing the interview scripts. In this process, you and your peer reviewer will focus on similarities as well as differences among the interviews and then come to a consensus of the overall codes and themes.

A Mixed Methods Approach

The mixed methods approach to dissertation research refers to the integration of both quantitative and qualitative research methods within a single study. It involves collecting and analyzing both numerical survey data (quantitative) and non-numerical (qualitative) interview responses to address research questions and hypotheses more comprehensively and gain a deeper understanding of the research topic.

In a mixed methods dissertation, you combine the strengths of quantitative and qualitative approaches to overcome the limitations of each method and provide a more holistic view of the research problem. By employing a mixed methods approach, you can gather both statistical data and rich narratives, allowing for a more nuanced and comprehensive analysis. This strategy allows you to capitalize on the strengths of both approaches. It also offers a deeper exploration of complex phenomena, a richer understanding of participant experiences, and greater strength to the overall validity and reliability of your findings.

One of the most beneficial aspects of employing a mixed methods approach is that your findings are integrated at the interpretation stage. This is where you look for patterns, relationships, or convergence/divergence between the two types of data and develop a more complete and robust understanding of the research problem and plausible solutions.

Summary and Concluding Comments

Chapter 3 of your dissertation is the roadmap of your research. By taking you from describing your research design, to defining your selection/recruitment process for participants, to communicating the data collection process, to addressing the data analysis plan, to conveying your approach to establishing validity and reliability, and finally to articulating the ethical considerations employed by your research – Chapter 3 becomes your dissertation compass and roadmap.

The essence of Chapter 3 is to introduce the items above and set the stage for conducting and analyzing your research in Chapters 4 and 5. The specific structure and content of Chapter 3 may vary depending on: your field of research, the nature of the study, and the dissertation guidelines provided by your academic institution and your dissertation chair. It is crucial that you consult the specific guidelines of your program to ensure you address all necessary requisites of your methodology chapter. The approaches contained herein are, by no means comprehensive; they are offered to give you a sense of how to approach a dissertation.

So with your roadmap in hand, it's time to visit the heart and soul of your manuscript – Chapters 4 and 5; this is where the serious work begins to get the heart pumping!

Chapter 8

So Where's the Beef? It's In Your Results, Findings, and Recommendations!

"Chapter 4 is the heart of the dissertation, where the researcher presents the findings of the study in a clear and systematic manner. It is the culmination of months or even years of data collection and analysis, providing the evidence to support the research questions and hypotheses."
— *Kathleen McMillan and Jonathan Weyers*

"Chapter 5 serves as a springboard for the next phase of scholarly engagement, inspiring other researchers to build upon the study's findings. It is the chapter that sparks curiosity and invites readers to continue the scholarly conversation, ultimately advancing knowledge in the field."
— *David Sternberg*

Chapter 4 is the part of your dissertation journey that describes the procedures you employed to analyze the data you have collected. It explains the techniques used to process, interpret, and make sense of the data. If you are doing quantitative research, it includes the statistical analyses – which may contain quantitative approaches related to the descriptive statistics associated with charts and graphs. For qualitative research, it addresses a thematic analysis, content analysis, or other qualitative approaches. You will also discuss the steps you have taken to ensure the validity and reliability of the study. This may consist of measures to enhance internal validity (e.g., control of variables) and external validity (e.g., sampling techniques to enhance generalizability). In chapter 5 you will also address potential sources of bias and limitations of your research. Additionally, you will indicate the steps you have taken to avoid introducing personal bias, and you will comment on the limits of your research. For example, considering only one geographic area for your research limits the implications of your work to a specific geographic area. Additionally, limiting research to just one specific area of consideration, such as information technology, creates a restriction to other areas of industry.

Chapters 4 and 5 of your dissertation present the findings and inherent meanings of your research. Not unlike a mystery novel, these chapters emphasize the intrigue, suspense, and fascination associated with unraveling a complex puzzle. It is this element of mystery and suspense that keeps readers engaged and eager to solve the puzzle alongside the protagonist. Chapter 4 of a dissertation typically focuses on presenting the results and findings of the research study. This chapter is commonly referred to as the "Results" or "Findings" chapter. Its purpose is to provide a comprehensive and detailed account of the data you collected during the research process and to analyze and interpret your findings in relation to the research questions or hypotheses.

The content of these chapters may vary depending on the research methodology you employed. If you are doing a quantitative or mixed methods study, you will begin with the presentation of the collected data, often in the form of descriptive statistics such as tables, graphs, or charts and then proceed to statistical analyses via Correlation, Chi Square, t-Test, Anova, etc. In addition, if you are engaged in qualitative research, you may have descriptive statistics that you would like to present, such as age or gender groupings, income stratifications, etc. When you are including graphs, charts, or tables, be sure you also offer a narrative description of the content. This data should be organized and clearly presented to facilitate understanding. An analysis and interpretation of your findings follow. This is the fun part where you look for trends and relationships in your data!

Here again, you will articulate your research questions and hypotheses, as well as your findings. These chapters are the chapters that provide a complete discussion of your findings because they explore the significance of your research, the implications, and the overall limitations of your study. Please keep in mind that speaking to the limitations of your research does not diminish it in any way – it actually provides an opportunity for other researchers to continue your fine work! During the process of authoring, you will relate the findings back to the gaps in the existing literature and your theoretical framework. Most important of all is to highlight any unique or noteworthy findings.

As you articulate your findings, if you are using a qualitative or mixed methods approach, you should include relevant quotations from your participants as well as excerpts from your interviews or textual survey responses. Warning; don't go overboard with this.

I have known dissertation writers to include every response from every participant. In fact, I have seen single quotations that ran multiple pages! It is important for you to extract verbiage from your interviews that specifically addresses the questions at hand. Be sure to employ specific intent and, by all means, do not include ramblings!

As you move into Chapter 5, you will offer a broader discussion and conclusions. Additionally, in order to maintain objectivity, you should acknowledge and discuss any limitations or delimitations that may have influenced your research. This shows your awareness of the constraints of your research and provides a necessary context for interpreting your overall results. You should conclude with a summary of the main findings, emphasizing their significance and contribution to your research.

Please note that all too often, dissertation authors forget to look back to their research questions to see if they have actually answered those questions! In academia, we call this the rabbit hole effect! Doctoral students seem to be constantly reacting to the newest shiny object! Keep yourself focused and review your research questions and/or hypotheses and articulate whether the data you collected either supports or refutes the questions and/or hypotheses.

Your objective in this dissertation journey is to find a "there-there" – if you do not find it, you have failed in your journey. "Your mission, should you choose to accept it," is to answer your research questions and/or hypotheses! I encourage my dissertation students to create a matrix that crosswalks research questions with findings. This offers a clear and specific way to see if the research questions have actually been answered!

Summary

Overall, the 4th chapter of a dissertation is the supreme inflection point where you present and analyze your research findings. This chapter is critical to providing a clear and thorough understanding of the data you collected and the implications of that data, with the ultimate goal of contributing to the overall body of knowledge in your chosen topic. According to John Creswell, it is in Chapter 4 that the researcher unveils the story that the data tells and offers a rich and detailed analysis of the findings. It is where research comes to life with vivid descriptions, meaningful interpretations, and compelling insights.[17]

You have arrived! Chapter 5 is the culmination of your efforts and should be designed to encourage others to continue your scholarly pursuits! It is where you present the conclusions and recommendations of your research. It is also the point at which you are able to say, "I have arrived as a researcher and as a scholar!" And perhaps, most importantly, this is the starting point for you to become Doctor Famous!!!

In addition, this is the chapter where you reflect on your research journey by summarizing the key findings and drawing conclusions that answer the research questions. It is also the chapter where you demonstrate the significance of your work and the contribution it makes to your field of study. Chapter 5 is the space for reflection and synthesis. It is where you step back and offer a holistic understanding of your research. It is the space in which you put a stake in the ground and offer recommendations for future research and practice. This is where you highlight the limitations of your research, acknowledge areas for improvement, and pave the way for others to build upon the exploration you have begun. For when it's all said and done, the true purpose of your research is to lay the groundwork of advancing knowledge!

Chapter 9

TIME TO TAKE A BOW!

"The [final] dissertation defense is a transformative experience, where the researcher transitions from a student to a scholar. It is a moment of intellectual independence, where they have the opportunity to present their research, receive feedback, and engage with experts in their field, ultimately shaping their future trajectory as a researcher."

— Chris M. Golde

Perhaps nothing in a doctoral program is as intimidating as a defense. During your dissertation journey, you will defend twice: once for your proposal, and once for the final defense of your entire manuscript. There are good reasons you may feel anxious and afraid, threatened, and downright paranoid about defending your dissertation. There are many reasons for this! First of all, if things don't go well, you may have wasted years of hard work. But perhaps equally important is the fact that your academic ego is at stake.

No one likes being judged, and your position in front of your dissertation chair and committee is all about judgement. Remember, these individuals will be attesting, with their signatures, that your research is worthy of publication. So keep in mind that this is about them as well as it is about you. No doubt, you will be concerned that your work is "good enough" – and that's okay because it happens to every doctoral candidate! Keep your cool and offer the best defense presentations you can possibly give.

There are two times during your dissertation journey where you will be in the spotlight defending your work. The first time is when you defend your proposal. Your dissertation proposal addresses the first three chapters of your manuscript. These chapters are the Introduction, the Literature Review, and the Methodology Chapters. The defense of your proposal needs to establish the problem you are addressing along with the associated research questions. It needs to confirm that there is a gap in the research literature that establishes the need for your study. Additionally, the proposal defense articulates the approach you will use in your study (quantitative, qualitative, or mixed methods). You will also speak to ethical considerations as well as the interface with the IRB.

Your proposal defense will include creating your slide deck, editing the deck over and over again, double-checking the consistency between your first three chapters and the deck, and practicing the presentation over and over again! My custom when chairing proposal defenses is to conduct "dress rehearsals" with my students. Doing this reduces the stress of the proposal defense on the student. You might consider requesting a dress rehearsal from your dissertation chair. It will give you an idea of what your chair may ask during the defense and overall reduce your fears of presenting. Keep in mind that the defense of your proposal is critical since it offers your path to obtaining IRB approval and the authorization for subsequent research.

I would be remiss not to include that many times during a proposal defense, you may encounter someone who has suggestions on "other things" you should add to your research. This can be so deflating since you have spent an inordinate amount of time selectively paring down your research to create a focused and concentrated approach to your topic. Nonetheless, and believe it or not, these suggestions are really an opportunity for you to begin building your Chapter 5! One of the areas of Chapter 5 is Recommendations for Future Research. So take the suggestions of well-meaning committee members and colleagues, thank them, and let them know that you will be using their ideas in your recommendations for future research.

Your second defense is the final defense of the dissertation and is an anxiety-ridden challenge that requires significant preparation. This is the last big hurdle, and your preparation time will be much more time-consuming and intense than what you have invested to date. While you should have been spending approximately 90 minutes per day authoring your manuscript, preparing for your final defense will be more like eight hours each day! Similar to your proposal defense, it will include creating your slide deck, editing the deck over and over again, double-checking the consistency between your manuscript and the deck, and practicing the presentation over and over again! Barbara E. Lovitts describes the dissertation defense as "a pivotal moment in a researcher's journey, where they have the opportunity to present their work, engage in scholarly discourse, and demonstrate their expertise in the field. It is a culmination of their hard work and an exciting step towards becoming a contributing member of the academic community."

Fortunately, there are tactics you can employ to keep your cool during the defense process. One of these is simply to do the prep work. Just like in real estate where the critical word is location-location-location; for a dissertation defense the critical word is preparation-preparation-preparation! If you experience glossophobia (fear of public speaking) I encourage you to read "Mesmerize: How to Give Your Best Presentation Ever" by yours truly!

On a similar note, be sure to practice-practice-practice. As with the proposal defense, prior to the final defense, I have my students do a "dress rehearsal" with me. Once again, this is not only good for practice, but you can gain insight into how your chair will act during your final defense. This approach allows your nerves to settle, ensures your presentation tracks with your manuscript, and have a chance to answer "live" questions from your chair. Without fail, my students have been thankful for this. If you have the opportunity to do a dress rehearsal with your dissertation chair, please do so!

According to Patricia Goodson, it is important to keep in mind that "The dissertation defense is not merely an examination of the research; it is a celebration of intellectual growth and achievement. It is a platform where the researcher demonstrates their ability to think critically, articulate their ideas, and defend their findings, all while engaging in a rigorous academic dialogue."

It is interesting to note, according to Joan Bolker, "the dissertation defense is not just about proving oneself to the committee; it is about sharing knowledge, engaging in intellectual debate, and contributing to the advancement of the field. It is an opportunity for the researcher to demonstrate their ability to bridge theory and practice and make a meaningful impact through their research."

Kamala London shares, "the dissertation defense is both a challenging and rewarding experience. It is a culmination of years of hard work, dedication, and perseverance. It is a moment to showcase the researcher's expertise, resilience, and growth as a scholar. Ultimately, it is an affirmation of their readiness to contribute to the academic community and make a difference in their chosen field."

In a nutshell, what are the most important actions you can take to effectively prepare to defend? First off, on the day of the defense, manage your anxiety by practicing relaxation techniques, such as deep breathing or visualization exercises. Deep breathing exercises, meditation, or mindfulness practices can help center your mind and reduce anxiety. Additionally, engaging in physical activity or taking breaks to relax and clear your mind can be beneficial.

Secondly, dress professionally and arrive early to familiarize yourself with the environment. Maintain a confident and composed demeanor during the defense, even if you encounter challenging questions or critique. Thorough preparation is key to feeling confident and composed during your defense. Know your research inside out, anticipate potential questions, and practice your presentation multiple times. The more prepared you are, the more at ease you'll feel. Remember that the panel members are interested in evaluating your work; they are not trying to undermine you.

As an additional strategy, try thinking ahead of the questions you might be asked. One of my students took great pains to assemble a comprehensive list of possible questions he might be asked in the course of his defense. Quite frankly, he went overboard – with more than 100 prep questions! Nonetheless, as you prepare, consider potential questions that the panel may ask and prepare thoughtful and concise responses.

Also, note that visualization can win the day! One of the most important actions you can take is to visualize yourself giving a dynamic and persuasive presentation. Close your eyes and see yourself before your committee with poise and confidence. Picture yourself fielding questions with calm assurance and effectively explaining your research findings. All told, visualizing success with your defense can help reduce your anxiety and build a positive mindset. Please be aware that you can project confidence through your body language, tone of voice, and delivery. Maintain eye contact with the committee members, speak clearly and concisely, and use confident gestures. Even if you feel nervous internally, projecting confidence externally can help you maintain a sense of calm and professionalism.

When the time comes for the "big day," be open to constructive criticism and demonstrate your ability to defend and support your research decisions and findings. Be sure to listen intently to the questions and comments from the panel members during your defense. Pause and take a moment to understand your committee's perspective before responding. Engage in a respectful and thoughtful discussion that showcases your knowledge and expertise. And above all, be open to alternative points of view and express your ability to engage in scholarly discourse. Do not, I repeat, do not, become defensive and argumentative!

During both your proposal and final defenses, engage with your committee; after all, your committee is there to support you and provide constructive feedback. You can engage with them during your defenses by actively listening to their questions, seeking clarification if needed, and responding thoughtfully. Approach each defense as a collaborative conversation rather than a confrontational situation. Take note that during a defense it is okay to say, "I don't know," if you genuinely don't have an answer to a question. This is far better than creating a "bullshit rhetorical" response to something you simply do not know. Also, be willing to engage in a productive dialogue with the panel. And above all, keep in mind that no one on your committee knows more about your topic than you do! Remember, defending your dissertation is a significant milestone, and you have already demonstrated your capabilities throughout your research journey. Trust in your expertise, stay composed, and believe in the value of your work.

Summary

Regardless of the outcome of your defense, be sure to reflect on your experience and learn from it. Carefully consider the feedback you received concerning areas for improvement. As you make the required revisions, see them as the path to further strengthen your work. Most importantly, stay focused on the big picture, i.e. the significance and value of your research. Keep in mind the contributions you are making to your field of study and the knowledge you've gained throughout your dissertation journey. Doing this can help you maintain your sense of purpose and your perspective during the process.

Embrace this phase of your doctoral journey as a learning opportunity. This will allow you to shift your perspective and view the defense process as an opportunity to engage in scholarly discourse, receive valuable feedback, and enhance your understanding of your research topic. Ultimately, this perspective can help alleviate pressure and foster a more positive mindset for you.

Stay focused on your "WHY" and "keep your eyes on the prize" noting the significance and value of your research and the contributions you are making to your field and the knowledge you've gained throughout your academic journey. By focusing on the importance of your work, you can maintain a sense of just how important your research is to the body of knowledge.

By all means, keep in mind that defending your dissertation is the culmination of your hard work and expertise. By thorough preparation, practice, and even meditation, you can ready yourself for an incredible success. Even though the results (good or bad) of your dissertation defenses can have far-reaching effects, it is paramount to remember that you have done your very best. That is all you can expect of yourself!

Part III

Tricks of the Trade: What Your Professors Didn't Share!

Chapter 10

BRINGING YOUR DISSERTATION INTO THE WORLD

"To achieve great things, two things are needed: a plan, and not quite enough time."

— Leonard Bernstein

When it comes right down to it, there is nothing like a sense of urgency to get a task done! How often do we wait until the last minute to even begin a project? If you are like most of us, this is certainly the case for your dissertation. Relying on any or all the tips below can help you bridge the gap between your "as is" state and your "to be" goal. Just take a brief moment to examine exactly where you are in your dissertation journey. Have you defended your proposal? Have you even chosen a topic? The ideas presented below are designed to help you address where you are and how to complete your dissertation journey as easily and quickly as possible. So put on your seatbelt and get ready to go from "urgency" to "done." Frequently consider the adage, *the best dissertation is a done dissertation!*

Welcome To The World of "Solopreneurship"!

Yep, you heard right! Your life as a dissertation creator is very much akin to being a solopreneur. It is your job to curate your research into a symphony of melodic information. However, very early in the journey, you realize this is not what you expected it would be. You soon realize you must do this almost 100% on your own. One of the most common misgivings among dissertation students is the amount of support to expect from your chair. Let me tell you from experience as someone who has written and successfully defended a dissertation, and chaired countless dissertations, your dissertation chair is NOT your personal proofreader, your editor, your researcher, your psychologist, or your Mom! Your dissertation chair is there to guide you in discussions, answer questions, offer suggestions, and help you stay on a reasonable timeline. Perhaps most importantly, your chair is there to try to keep you from going down rabbit holes!

Where business solopreneurs are fundamentally responsible for balancing their work and their time, so too, producing your dissertation means that you are the sole operator of this project and that you must handle multiple responsibilities simultaneously. And like a solopreneur, the boundary between work and personal life will probably blur for you, often resulting in challenges with maintaining a healthy work-life balance. Juggling multiple facets of your dissertation and being solely responsible for its success can lead to burnout and feelings of overwhelm.

And to compound matters, here you sit with limited resources. After all, you have already spent most of your money on tuition and books! So at this point, it may be difficult, if not impossible, to invest in an editor or a full-service academic consulting firm. As mentioned above, and worse yet, this journey can lead to feelings of isolation and a lack of social interaction, where you will find your motivation and overall well-being impacted. This can have a deleterious effect on a process that requires you to make critical decisions across various aspects of research, authoring, and defending your manuscript.

While all these challenges will be quite overwhelming, you can overcome them by seeking support from friends, family, and at times, psychologists. By leveraging technology and focusing on self-care, you are more likely to adapt to the rigor and requirements of the dissertation. Keep your focus and know that this journey is, albeit taxing, finite in duration.

As a footnote, one story I found touching was about cohort connectedness and concerned a young lady who was experiencing health issues, specifically cancer. Her cohort rallied around her, but unfortunately, while she was finishing her dissertation, she passed. In an act of love, her cohort went on to finish writing her dissertation. It was published posthumously. Such is the power of creating and keeping relationships. So keep in contact with your cohort during and after your doctoral journey. It won't take much time – just a simple text will do the trick to keep you connected. These are people you can rely on for emotional support during dissertation and for making future contact with others in your field.

Health and Well-Being

Writing a dissertation can have a significant impact on your health and well-being. I'm sure you are thinking, "how can this be bad for my health?" Just take some time to consider the following. First, the dissertation process can be stressful and anxiety-inducing. In the initial weeks of your dissertation, you need to come to terms with the fact that your dissertation will intrude on your life as you know it. Be ready for this! Do not permit this journey to interfere with your health.

The intense and prolonged nature of writing a dissertation can take its toll on your physical and mental health. You may experience symptoms of depression, anxiety, and burnout associated with the dissertation journey. In addition, you will have pressure to meet deadlines set by your dissertation chair. This can cause disruptions in your sleep. Yet another area to consider is that the dissertation process may lead to poor nutrition. You may be skipping meals, or worse yet, overeating junk foods, which can negatively impact your energy levels, overall well-being, and cause significant weight gain or loss. This coupled with long hours of sitting while working at your computer can easily lead to back pain, neck strain, and decreased overall fitness (consider buying and using a stand-up desk!).

Yet another stressor is money! As each term ticks by, you know your academic debt is increasing. Meet this head-on by knowing what your debt is, and will be, by the time you graduate. Putting your head in the sand will not make the financial challenge go away. Take the time to acknowledge the impact on your finances. Since it is your goal to have a doctoral degree, like many things in life, you must pay for it (now or later). Overall, the level of stress this can induce is significant.

So what's a dissertation writer to do? Perhaps more important than anything else is to stay healthy! You may think that you have no time to exercise, and in the traditional sense you are correct. You do not have time to be a gym rat. However, and this is an important however, you *do* have time to walk away from your computer or even take a walk outside for a brief period. What's great about taking a brief walk is that it not only gives you some exercise, but it also allows you to keep the blood flowing to your brain so you can think through some of the issues associated with your dissertation. Even a simple stretch break will re-energize you. And if you find yourself experiencing significant mental health challenges in coping with the demands of your dissertation journey, seek professional help. Do not hesitate to find a therapist to assist you. Realizing this in advance can go a long way to helping you cope.

Making your health a priority may seem an impossible goal. Know that you are not alone in this. In fact, for most doctoral students health is not a priority since they believe they do not have the time to add even one more action to a daily to-do list! Be that as it may, let's take a look at some relatively simple and quick tactics that may work for you.

Over the years, the following tactics have helped my dissertation students. First off, drink water! According to the National Library of Medicine, hydration does more than benefit your physical wellness; it can also work wonders for your focus and alertness. Research indicates that even mild dehydration, defined as a body water loss of just 1-2%, can have a very real negative impact on your cognitive performance![18]

Second, eat right! Eating protein can help keep you healthy. I find getting a good dose of egg whites in the morning can go a long way to keep me full. Please don't think of this as distasteful or boring. I find all I need to do is "dress up" the egg whites with something special like pico de gallo, cheese for savoriness, or even vanilla protein powder for some sweetness. Later in the day, salads topped with tuna or ground turkey casserole can keep you calm and full. And when you want to reach for a sweet treat, reach for fruit!

In addition to healthy eating, a tactic that works wonders for both body and mind is meditation. Aside from reducing stress and anxiety, meditation lifts your mood and your overall well-being. There is a wide variety of methods to use for meditating, and they are well worth your time to research. Once you begin a practice of meditation, you will find your self-awareness, your creativity, and even your problem-solving skills will improve. Each day, as you work on your dissertation, consider meditating as your personal stress-reduction break!

Another helpful tactic is to find a dissertation buddy to help get you through the daily dissertation grind. Use the strong relationships you have built with your fellow doctoral students – after all, once you leave the "litter" in the classroom, your doctoral colleagues are the only people who can really understand what you are going through. Even though other people in your life will seem sympathetic, the people who can really understand are your doctoral colleagues! Authoring a dissertation is a unique experience, and unless someone you know is writing or has written a dissertation, they have no clue what you are doing.

Also, as mentioned earlier, recruiting an accountability partner can be an incredible strategy to both ease the stress and move your dissertation forward. Engaging an accountability partner can reduce your stress just by letting you know there is someone "out there" who cares enough to take this journey with you! This is the person with whom you can check in periodically (at least weekly) to discuss what you have accomplished on your dissertation in the past week and what you intend to accomplish in the following week. Be sure to set specific goals, for example, identifying milestones such as finding three or four peer-reviewed journal articles to review. The size of these targets can vary depending on how you define the next tactic – committing to a set amount of time each day to work on your dissertation. What has worked quite well for my best students was a personal pledge of 90 minutes per day. The amount of time you commit to the dissertation each day will drive the overall size and impact of your weekly goals.

And while we are on the topic of a time pledge, take a moment to identify your optimal time of day. This optimal time is the part of the day in which you are at your best to concentrate, research, and write. For me, it is the early-early hours of the day. I can accomplish three times as much from 5:00am to 6:30am than I can during the late morning or early afternoon. This is the time when I am not distracted by calls, messages, or people; it is when I am at my intellectual best.

Other Tactics Worth Considering

Music – Think about using headphones to listen to soothing music or even nature sounds. Music is a universal language that can positively affect people on various levels. Research suggests that you play music with 60-70 beats per minute, like Beethoven's Für Elise, which is known to help students study longer and retain more information. Additionally, the volume of your study music is a key consideration. Don't drown out your own thoughts with music that is too loud. As a final note about music – it should be in the background, so avoid music with commercials.[19]

Friends and Family – spending quality time with your support system can be a powerful way to recharge and boost your well-being. The people who care about you can provide the emotional support and connection that are essential for your mental and emotional health. While this could take too much of your valuable dissertation time, a reasonable timeframe of a 30-minute get-together can be well worth it.

Desk Exercises – When you are at your desk, try incorporating some simple exercises such as leg lifts, neck stretches, or shoulder rolls. These moves can help prevent muscle tension, and they are a great way to break up the monotony of the dissertation process. One of my favorite "healthy balance" tactic is to take short one-minute breaks – I call them one-minute wonders! After just one of these, I feel less stressed and so recharged!

Clear the Clutter – Maintain an organized and clutter-free workspace. Statistics also show that a clean workspace can increase your motivation by a significant 84%. Research says clutter prevents you from focusing on what you're doing. Our brains can only keep track of a few things at a time; therefore, clutter can hinder your focus, your motivation, and your productivity.[20]

Watch out for the Fear Factor! – And while you are keeping tabs on your health and well-being, be equally aware of how fear may be permeating your world, both fear of failure and even fear of success! All too often and in many situations, fear of failure or fear of success can play a destructive role in keeping us from achieving our goals.

The Fear of Success – Fear of success is a psychological phenomenon where individuals experience anxiety, apprehension, or resistance towards achieving their goals and realizing success. While fear of failure is more common, fear of success can be equally powerful and have a significant impact on personal and professional growth. Fear of success often stems from self-doubt and perfectionistic tendencies, where you may worry about whether you can meet the expectations that come with success.

Fear of success can be the #1 factor keeping you from achieving your dissertation goals – don't let it affect your confidence! As you begin authoring your dissertation, you may become overwhelmed with a fear of success. But how can this possibly be? You have taken all your required doctoral courses and have passed them with flying colors! Now, all of a sudden, you have become fearful of completing this degree. Such a fear can stem from the anticipation of achieving the high expectations from your friends, family, and even yourself! And then you begin to anticipate a harrowing pressure to maintain that level of success. This intense fear and paranoia can manifest as self-doubt, perfectionism, or a fear of the unknown. As a result, you may become overwhelmed, procrastinate, or experience imposter syndrome, where you question your abilities and begin to feel undeserving of success. Such a fear can undermine your confidence, hinder your progress, and even diminish the motivation you need to complete your dissertation in a timely manner – or even at all!

Fear of Failure – As is the case with most dissertation students, you may experience strong concerns about criticism. You may fear being judged, criticized, or even envied by others. This, in turn, can create anxiety and reluctance to pursue your goal of completing your dissertation.

Overcoming the fear of success and the fear of failure requires you to take proactive steps to address these fears. So challenge your negative beliefs, ask for support from your mentors, and set realistic goals. And simply tell yourself to – just stay in your dissertation writing chair one more day! Above all, keep in mind, you are good enough to do this, or you wouldn't be here! Don't take yourself too seriously. You are smart enough and you are worthy! If fear is the #1 factor keeping you from achieving your dissertation goals – don't let it attack your confidence!

Make your Self-Talk Work for You – Above all, be mindful of your self-talk. How you treat yourself mentally is just as important as how you care for your physical well-being. You need to be your own best friend during this time – so be just that. Use self-talk that emphasizes how far you have come, the incredible quality of the work you are creating, and what you will produce in your completed dissertation! **YOU GOT THIS!!!**

Psychological Hiccups
AKA Psychological Avoidance

All too often students seem to take FOREVER to complete their dissertations. This is generally characterized as simple procrastination (more on this later!) However, along the lines of procrastination is the distant and pesky first cousin known as the psychology of avoidance. The psychology of avoidance is most commonly known as the "quick fix" to a feeling of discomfort – and it is, in fact, an extremely effective way to avoid what you just don't want to do. For example, if you are dieting and hunger sets in, it's uncomfortable, right? Unfortunately, the discomfort, i.e. hunger pangs, can easily lead you to avoid your diet plan all together! Or have you ever dashed off an email response in anger without considering the ultimate consequences? These situations reflect the psychological avoidance of trying to eliminate discomfort or control distress and often make matters worse!

Lurking in all of us is psychological avoidance. Sometimes we put off making a phone call, other times we may avoid paying a bill, and even more often we avoid what could be a constructive discussion with a friend, fearing that it may lead to conflict. Whatever the reason, avoiding situations, decisions, and appropriate actions can bring us to anxiety and actually make matters worse. Avoiding certain social situations can lead to isolation; deferring a decision to see a doctor can result in negative health impacts; and not taking action on your dissertation can result in you not obtaining your doctoral degree. And though psychological avoidance may bring us momentary relief emotionally, quite frequently, it carries with it, a steep cost. Some people refer to psychological avoidance as "burying your head in the sand." The bad news is that this avoidance can be fatal, causing us to run out of emotional oxygen. However, the good news is that there are ways to change the avoidance "habit." The first step is just to recognize it![21]

"Remaining" is a specific type of psychological avoidance. It occurs when someone remains in a situation to avoid the discomfort of change. This occurs frequently in a relationship where someone knows the relationship is not good, but they can't bring themselves to break it off.

Yet another type of avoidance is "retreating". This is often the case with dissertation students who feel so anxious by the daunting task ahead of them that they actually stop opening their manuscript file, trying to make the anxiety go away. In certain cases, some students have stopped working on their manuscripts altogether, believing their fear of public speaking will overtake them during their final defense and render them failures! Ultimately, retreat avoidance can keep you from completing your degree program and remain ABD (All But Dissertation).[22]

All told, psychological avoidance feels good in the moment, but it comes with the burden of increased anxiety because the root cause of the avoidance remains. Since you do not have the luxury to lag when writing your dissertation, it is important for you to get a grip on this. You must keep moving forward in the knowledge that there are some methods that can help you overcome avoidance.

Consider some of these approaches to assist you in this daunting task. First and foremost, when a situation presents with anxiety, it's time to evaluate your thoughts rather than simply reacting. Actually take the time to debate with yourself and challenge your thoughts, ideas, and feelings. Try the "someone else" approach by asking yourself what you would say to counsel a friend in the same situation. Then take another look at the situational anxiety that is causing your stress.[23] For your dissertation, think of the advice and encouragement you would give a fellow student who is in the same boat!

Another approach is to just "jump in!" Go ahead and just open your dissertation file. That's all that you need to do with your first step – open the damn file! Now breathe and pat yourself on the back. Remember to tell yourself that only very small steps are needed to begin a process and think of the quotation from the Chinese philosopher Lao Tzu: "The journey of a thousand miles begins with one step." Make this your mantra; after all, you won't get anywhere unless you begin. Remember to take baby steps when you are beset by dissertation anxiety and psychological avoidance – just open the file – write 100 words – find one peer-reviewed journal article. Baby steps!

A final suggestion I offer you when you find yourself experiencing psychological avoidance is to examine *what* you are avoiding in the context of your values, and ask yourself, "what does this degree mean to me?"[24] Remember the "why" discussion in the earlier part of this book? Keep in mind that your dissertation must matter to you. It must be aligned with what you value, or you wouldn't have begun a doctoral program in the first place. Examining what is important to you can reduce the anxiety of your dissertation. In sum, dealing with psychological avoidance in a dissertation is not about having courage or being fearless; it's more about not permitting the anxiety to rule your life and disable your dream.

Psychological Hiccups AKA Procrastination

Along the lines of psychological avoidance is the dreaded monster known as procrastination. Even though we have all heard "isms" such as "Don't put off until tomorrow, that which you can do today", or "Be sure to make hay when the sun shines", many, if not most of us, find it difficult to actually accomplish the most important (and even the most mundane) goals. As Abraham Lincoln said, "You cannot escape the responsibility of tomorrow by evading it today." Don't be the doctoral candidate who can't seem to complete a dissertation even though you managed to complete all the doctoral course requirements with flying colors!

Procrastination isn't a disease that we can catch or take a pill to cure. It is more of a symptom. It reveals itself in tasks you have completed late, the ones you've left unfinished, or worse, the ones you've totally abandoned! However, procrastination is less about the "undone" and more about the impact on our psyches, our feelings of self-esteem, and perhaps most shamefully, the impact to our reputations![25]

While there are parts of our brains that allow us to be logical, work through our emotions, and delay gratification, the monkey part is quite controlling and requires us to "counter-control" the problematic and procrastinating monkey brain. That means that we need to acquire and implement tools to assist us. When you have household projects to do, you use tools, right? You use screwdrivers, hammers, drills, etc. These tools make the task easier and, in fact, doable. So too, there are tools that can help us deal with procrastination.[26]

While creating your dissertation, addressing monkey brain procrastination is a complex task. To begin to deal with this issue, you can start by creating a plan before your monkey brain kicks in! So get to work as soon as possible to draft a personalized (after all, we are all different) plan. One of the best actionable components you could address is to recall the old question, "How do you eat an elephant? One bite at a time!" So focus on only one piece of the dissertation plan at a time – focus, focus, focus. Design a daily routine for yourself that works in concert with the time of day where you have your greatest mental acuity. As you address your routine day by day, you will build a discipline muscle to continue strong on this journey.[27] Ultimately, it is up to you to create a plan that works for you.

Please know that procrastination is a lurking constant during the dissertation process. It's around every corner and it is, in fact, a demon. Step one, acknowledge it! Then begin! Now set a short timer of 10 to 30 minutes and get going!

Time Flies – So Manage It Wisely!

It never ceases to amaze me how students begin the dissertation journey with the belief that it will be a short-term endeavor, only to find out that one semester leads into another and they are befuddled that they have made little progress. The fact is that without employing one or more of the tools of time management, days turn into weeks, weeks turn into months, and months turn into years without making significant headway! The purpose of this section is to share the best practices of dissertation students who have come before you.

Consider Using An Intentions Log and a Project Management Tool

Much like taking a vacation by car, the first thing you need is your intended route. I like to see students complete an intentions log each week where they indicate the three actions they accomplished the previous week and the three actions they will take in the coming week. Obviously, your first week of filling out your intentions log will not include the prior week's actions. A copy of the template for your intentions log is included in Appendix D, along with a sample log that has been filled out for you as an example. I have found using this approach to be quite helpful for just about any multi-week/month project.

A great way to decide which tasks to prioritize is by using a project management (Appendix C) chart. You can put all your dissertation tasks here, decide the dates by which you plan to complete them, and sort as necessary. This guides your decision-making process as to what to do and when to do it.

Your Goals Drive Your Results, So Be SMART!

As you create your intentions log and project management plan, examine your entries from the vantage point of evaluating if your goals are "SMART." You're probably familiar with the idea of SMART[28] goals, so here is a brief review. This process is critical to efficient and effective time management. When it's all said and done, SMART intentions can give you the focus and motivation to go on and succeed. When you know where the goal line is, you'll want to work to achieve it and even beat it. Your smart goals can become the challenging force to take you out of your comfort zone and into the end-zone!

The "**S**" of **S**MART goals means that your goals are **specific** in as much as they need to be clear. As an example, stating that you are going to work on your lit review is not specific. It needs to explicitly state, for example, that you are going to find and summarize ten journal articles that offer direct relevance to your dissertation topic. The "S" is where you clearly state the action(s) you will accomplish.

The "**M**" of SMART intentions speaks to **measurability** and the need for you to use numbers when stating your goals. In the previous example, note that I used the number "ten" as a measurable part of the intention. It is critical that you include a quantifiable objective in your intentions so that you are able to track your progress and get an idea of just where you are on the journey.

As for the "**A**" in SMART, this addresses **achievability** where you need to feel confident and believe that you are being realistic in setting the intention. This is where you can ask yourself, "on a scale of one to ten, how confident am I that I can achieve this goal?" If your answer is in the range of one to seven, redefine your goal. If you find that a goal for your timeframe is too big of a stretch, break the goal into something smaller and more bite-sized! For example, a goal of writing your entire lit review in a day is not particularly doable. Instead, a goal of researching one or two relevant peer-reviewed journal articles in a day is far more achievable.

The "**R**" in SMART informs **relevance**. This is the place where you can check yourself to see if you are succumbing to "rabbit holes" and falling prey to the "next shiny thing!" Throughout your entire dissertation journey, there will be a persistent danger of expanding your research beyond what you intended. Hence, for each goal or intention, ask yourself if it meets the relevance test of being truly necessary and germane to your topic. An intention that entertains the concept of employee retention will most likely not support research into psychological support for neurodiverse clients. However, employee retention may certainly be directly related to employee training. As you evaluate intentions for relevance look for the direct benefit to your dissertation area.

The final letter, "**T**" is for **time-bound**. Each of your intentions should prescribe a specific deadline. Without a timely and specific target date, you are pretty much flailing about. The timeline allows you to evaluate your successes and establish follow-on intentions. This is where you set realistic deadlines for each task and assign deadlines. Breaking down larger projects into smaller milestones with clear deadlines, helps you to maintain your motivation. Hence, it is important to ensure your timelines are realistic so you can avoid unnecessary stress or compromise the quality of your work.

Put as simply as possible:

A goal without a deadline is *fantasy*.

A goal with a deadline is an *objective*.

A goal with a deadline and a plan is an *intention*.

A goal with a deadline, a plan, and consistent action is *success*.

A *personal meaningful goal* with a deadline, a plan, and consistent action is *fulfillment!*[29]

However, try as you might, life happens, and all of your plans may need to be sidelined when the unexpected occurs. It is not unusual for dissertation students to face life events that delay accomplishing their goals. These events can include illness, divorce, marriage, birth of a child, loss of a job, etc. Any of these life events can impact the completion of your dissertation.

In sum, it is interesting to note the single most frequent cause of "delay of game" is "procrastination-itis!" Hence, it is critical that time management be high on your list of skills to master.

Some Specific Tried-and-True Techniques for Managing Time

According to Seth Godin[30], "it's almost impossible to remove a screw with your bare hands, but easy with a screwdriver. The handle might only add a little torque, but it's more than enough. If someone is succeeding at something you find difficult, it might be because they realized they needed a screwdriver! Looking for the tool is the first step in finding it." What follows in this section is a series of tried and proven tools for managing your time and your dissertation. I have chosen these because I use them while advising the doctoral dissertation students I chair, and because they have saved both me and my students an incredible amount of time and frustration while successfully navigating the path to "doctorhood!"

There are a myriad of formalized and time-honored time management techniques. As for me, I tend to use a variety of them, so I don't become burned out by using just one. I also find ways of using two or more of the techniques simultaneously. So feel free to vary your usage of these tools to ultimately increase your effectiveness on your dissertation journey. Regardless of the techniques you choose to use, most important, work on your dissertation EVERYDAY! Yes, every day, including weekends and holidays! It really doesn't matter that you address the same elements every day, it matters that you open the file, set a timer, and work. Whether your goal is 25 minutes (the Pomodoro Technique) or a goal of 90 minutes every damn day, which is my preferred tool, just stick to your self-imposed goals.

One of the techniques that works well for me is the Pomodoro Technique[31], and is sometimes described as a time blocking system. For this approach, break your work time into a 25-5-25-15 interval protocol. This means that you work with focus (no interruptions) for 25 minutes, then you take a break for 5 minutes. After four iterations, then take a longer break of 15 minutes. This approach works to maintain focus by working in concentrated "chunks". By all means, do not fail to take these breaks. They are essential for maintaining your focus and preventing burnout while allowing you to recharge, stretch, and clear your mind.

It is important that during your timed work periods you have the latitude to decide what to work on. For example, during your scheduled "work times" you can find and read another journal article, you can research your school's requirements, you can delve into the software you will use to calculate statistical significance, categorize your qualitative results, or write a page. Surprisingly, you may find that each time you work on your dissertation, you are taken into "flow" – a state where you lose track of time and work even more than you originally intended!

Another approach that works especially well for me is the "Eat That Frog"[32] tactic! This time management method was created and coined by Brian Tracy. Tracy suggests that we attack our most challenging task first thing in the morning. This is particularly good for me since my most productive time of the day is early morning. If you are a night person, you may need to flip this one! However, the true advantage of using the early morning to eat that frog is that you get on a roll that enhances your momentum, moderates your procrastination, and gives you a whopping surge in productivity. What is really nice about this approach is that you can combine it with the Pomodoro technique and further boost your results. Nonetheless, it is up to you to determine your most productive time. Identify the time of day when you are most alert and productive. Schedule your most important and challenging tasks during this time to leverage your peak energy levels and focus.

The next technique that can work wonders for you is one that allows you to attend to your dissertation while addressing "life" issues. Unfortunately, life does not stop while you are creating and researching your dissertation! There remains laundry, bill paying, doctor visits, childcare, grocery shopping, even planning a wedding, having a baby; the list goes on and on. In addition, there are times when the unexpected happens – you or a member of your family become ill (sometimes seriously), you and your spouse decide to divorce, or you and/or your spouse lose your job(s). This is a time when the Eisenhower Matrix[33] can be quite useful. Named after the 34th President of the United States, it is a method for rank-ordering tasks that need to be accomplished. This technique is known as the Urgent-Important Matrix and is used to place your tasks into categories by quadrants: urgent and important, important but not urgent, urgent but not important, and not urgent and not important. The approach is also sometimes referred to as the ABC Method for classifying tasks by importance and urgency. The ABC comes in when individual actions are prioritized as "A" – high priority, "B" – moderate priority, and "C" – low priority.

Urgent and Important – Do It Now!	Important but not Urgent – Schedule It!
Urgent but not Important – Delegate It!	Not Urgent and Not Important – Eliminate It!

Please note that the first category of urgent and important in the Eisenhower matrix describes work that should be your #1 priority and should be addressed ASAP! While your dissertation is important, you should consider elements of it that involve meeting dates and attending interviews with your participants as urgent.

In the second quadrant of the matrix, important but not urgent, would include elements of your dissertation that are administrative by form and come under the heading of "this can wait." These tasks include file configuration and management, development of your table of contents, as well as viewing various technology YouTubes.

Tasks that can be rescheduled or delegated are considered in the third quadrant of urgent but not important. If possible, delegate tasks that can be handled by others, freeing up your time for more important responsibilities. Additionally, learn to say "NO" to tasks or commitments that do not align with your priorities or overload your schedule. If you must spend time on such tasks, be sure to work on them as quickly as possible and minimize the time you spend on such actions. As a dissertation example, consider using library personnel to find and order resources for you. While it is urgent that you obtain the resources, it is not important that you personally do the heavy lifting of locating said resources.

It is interesting that many of us like to attend to the fourth quadrant of the not urgent/not important tasks as they tend to be easy to do and we can quickly check them off our lists for a wonderful sense of immediate gratification! While you are working on your dissertation, do not fall victim to this.

For those of you who enjoy making lists (and who doesn't?) there is the Ivy Lee Method[34]. Lee was a productivity consultant, and as the story goes Lee was hired by the president of Bethlehem Steel Corp. in 1918. It has been documented that Lee crafted a deal where he would introduce a new methodology for increasing productivity. Lee's fee would be nothing unless productivity increased, and his consulting agreement stipulated that the Bethlehem executive would, at the end of the project, send him what he thought the service was worth. At the completion of the work, Lee received a check for $25,000. A $25,000 check written in 1918 is the equivalent of more than $450,000 in 2025!

All told, the Ivy Lee Method consists of creating a list of the six most important tasks you need to accomplish the following day in order of their priority. At the start of the next day, begin focusing on the first task on your list and continue to the second one, but only after you have finished the first task. This technique provides for ongoing focus throughout your efforts on completing the list and achieving enhanced efficiency. It is interesting to note that this approach is consistent with the Pareto Principle which states that 80% of your results come from 20% of your efforts. Identify the tasks or activities that yield the highest impact and prioritize them accordingly. Remember to focus on high-value tasks that align with your goals and have a significant impact on your desired outcomes.

Also worthy of note is a technique created by David Allen and is known as the GTD (Getting Things Done)[35] approach that involves capturing all tasks, clarifying their importance, organizing them into categories, regularly reflecting on progress, and taking action. This process helps maintain a clear mind, serves to manage tasks effectively, and keeps you on top of commitments. While this is not my favorite approach to use with a dissertation, it does have its merits. I urge caution using the GTD since it may put you in a state of overwhelm if you use it as an overall tool for your dissertation. Instead, if you choose to apply it, do it with just one area of the dissertation, such as defining your research methodology.

Alternatively, another tool you can employ during your dissertation journey is the Kanban Method[36]. The Kanban Method, often used in conjunction with a Kanban board, helps manage your tasks and the overall flow of your action items. It involves listing work elements into columns such as "To Do," "In Progress," and "Done." By visually representing tasks and progress, you gain insight into your workload so that you can manage your dissertation more effectively.

Finally, though the following technique is predominantly used in project management, Agile Methodology[37] is a time management approach that focuses on iterative and incremental work. This involves breaking your action items projects into small but manageable tasks and then prioritizing them based on your dissertation milestones and requirements. This is a technique where you regularly review and make adjustments (usually in conjunction with your dissertation chair) in order to ensure adaptability throughout the project.

Some Final Thoughts on Managing Your Time

As I complete our section regarding time management, one thing I want to emphasize is to avoid multitasking, as it can decrease productivity and lead to errors. If you feel you must address multiple action items that require little time, use something known as the two-minute rule. The two-minute rule was devised by David Allen and encourages that if something can be accomplished in two minutes or less, do it immediately[38]. I advocate for using this tool, especially on those occasions when you begin to feel overwhelmed by "a million little things," preying on your mind and virtually paralyzing you!

While I have offered you a virtual buffet of time-management tools and methodologies, now is the time to reiterate the #1 time waster and its antigen – rabbit holes and monk mode! Monk mode is a period of intense focus. It is where you eliminate distractions and address deep work. Fortunately, you can use monk mode to deal with the bane of the dissertation experience – rabbit holes. Working in monk mode is the perfect way of avoiding being sucked into these rabbit holes.

At the heart of rabbit holes are distractions. These distractions can range from deciding on what to have for a snack to getting up to vacuum your office! There are very few things that are so earth-shattering that you should allow them to interfere with your chosen dissertation time. In order to eliminate distractions from your work at hand, disable your electronic notifications, stay away from social media, and eliminate unnecessary internet browsing. Use website blockers or apps that limit your access to distracting websites during your focused work sessions. Place your phone in another room, put a "do not disturb" sign on your door, set specific goals for your dissertation session, and decide on the period of time you will remain undistractedly engaged.

Remember, monk mode is a tool to help you harness your deep focus, maximize your productivity, avoid those pesky rabbit holes, and make the most of your dissertation time. Don't get sucked into rabbit holes!

Yet another and quite dangerous aspect of rabbit holes (and one we have discussed earlier) involves researching other ideas about your dissertation that happen to pop into your head. Most often, these ideas come under the heading of "wouldn't it be nice to research ABC?" where ABC is a tangent to the real work at hand. Do not be suckered into researching the next "shiny thing" that bears virtually no resemblance to your topic! Simply write the idea down on a list for future research. This will take it off your mind and get you back on track.

Chapter 11

CREATING YOUR DREAM TEAM

"Teams are incredible things. No task is too great, no accomplishment too grand, no dream too far-fetched for a team. It takes teamwork to make the dream work."

— John C. Maxwell

Your personal dream team consists of your chair, your editor, your peer reviewer, and your accountability partner. Your dissertation chair is your lifeline and plays a profoundly important role in your dissertation. Choose your chair (and committee members) wisely. Select a chair with whom you have a positive and strong relationship, as well as an overall sense of synergy. Your chair is your critic, advisor, consultant, and perhaps most importantly, your cheerleader. Trust your chair! Overall, one of the biggest threats you face with your chair is losing this person! The path to finding another chair is time-consuming. Additionally, depending on where you are in your journey, there can be considerable time associated with your chair coming up to speed with the state and content of your research. Don't lose your dissertation *chairperson* by taking too long to complete your manuscript – keep in mind chairs change jobs too! Changing dissertation chairs can cost you as much as 12-18 additional months! This holds true for your committee members as well. Stay in touch with them but remember decisions and final input come from your chair.

Additionally, hiring an editor will save you a great deal of heartache, anxiety, and time. While most doctoral students worry about writing their dissertations, there are a few who believe this is "just another paper." IT IS NOT! And there are even those who, worse yet, believe that their dissertation will be the "be all and end all" of publications and win a Nobel Prize!!! It will not!

Regardless of whether you think authoring a dissertation is a difficult or easy experience, be sure to find an editor who has actually edited dissertations! Stay away from editors who have only specialized in editing undergraduate papers. You will need an editor who knows and understands the extraordinary dissertation process and requirements. You will need this person regardless of how well you write and how much you know about technology (i.e. for tables, the Table of Contents, figures, APA formatting, etc.). Equally important is that you do not select a relative or your best friend. Obtaining objective feedback from these people can result in an essentially unedited manuscript! Unfortunately, and all too often, dissertation students are "un-schooled" in APA compliance. If your doctoral program did not demand that you author in concert with APA requirements, for sure you need an editor!

All of this can be stressful and frustrating. So, find a proficient editor who can offer you an extra set of eyes and considerable experience. If you find complying with APA guidelines is a source of angst, hire an editor familiar with editing for APA compliance to ensure your manuscript complies with the requirements of APA.

You have enough to worry about researching and writing your dissertation – APA issues should not be on the list.

A special consideration is to hire an editor with the understanding that the person will perform multiple iterations of editing. Since your manuscript will change during the research and authoring process, only hire a person who commits to editing your document multiple times. "One and done" will not suffice!

In addition to hiring an editor, you should also find a peer reviewer. This person has a very important role in establishing intercoder reliability for your qualitative research. Also, find an accountability partner – someone, anyone! Unlike your chair, peer reviewer, or committee members, this is a person with whom you should meet once a week to tell them what you accomplished last week and what you will accomplish in the coming week. The mere act of sharing your intentions with someone else creates a sense of commitment you make to them. Each week, as you implement your intentions, you will feel a sense of accomplishment that can drive you forward; and reporting your accomplishments to your accountability partner leaves you more energized to "attack" your intentions in the following week. Keep in mind, motivation comes and goes. But accountability keeps you moving even when you don't feel like it!

Part IV

TOOLS OF THE TRADE

Chapter 12

THE SWOT ANALYSIS!

"Cultivate a deep understanding of yourself – not only what your strengths and weaknesses are but also how you learn, how you work with others, what your values are, and where you can make the greatest contribution. Because only when you operate from strengths can you achieve true excellence."

— *Peter Drucker*

By this point in your life, you have probably created more than one SWOT Analysis – but more than likely, in a business setting. Your dissertation gives you another opportunity to use this tool to address your Strengths, Weaknesses, Opportunities, and Threats in writing your dissertation. What is particularly helpful with your SWOT is that you can review it each day to remain mindful of your dissertation position. As an example, consider the following statements you might include.

- Strengths – "I am more than capable of writing this dissertation because tenacity is one of my strengths."

- Weakness – "I must be cautious of veering away from working on my dissertation since there are many demands on my time in my life."

- Opportunity – "This dissertation paves the way for future promotions at work and the achievement of a personal goal."

- Threats – "Distractions are seemingly everywhere and can derail my dissertation progress – I must be wary of these and use the tools I have amassed to hold distractions at bay."

Now it's time to roll up your sleeves! Find a quiet space where you can think and be introspective. As you consider your strengths, identify what time of day is especially good for you to accomplish tasks that require academic thinking and academic action, such as research. Some people do their best work first thing in the morning; others are night owls and should schedule time late in the day to work on their dissertations.

Identifying Your Strengths

Identifying your strengths is important, so make a list of them. Are you tenacious and focused? Are you incredibly strategic? Are you well-organized? How about detail-oriented – for some of us this is a strength, and for others it is a weakness since it can allow us to get bogged down and spend too much time on a single component of the dissertation!

Once you have built your strengths list, keep it in your work area and review it every day! Take comfort in the fact that your strengths will get you through the dissertation process.

Also, take note of the fact that the opposite of each of your strengths can be a weakness. If you are quite organized, consider the person who is very disorganized. This is not only a weakness; it can be a curse. This is the person who loses files, doesn't take the time to create a system of archiving research sources, and forgets to include vital parts of the dissertation in their manuscript. Take pride in each of your strengths, knowing that without them, you can have weaknesses that will bring down your dissertation like a house of cards!

Identifying Your Weaknesses

Though most of us avoid pinpointing our weaknesses, this is a time when it is critical to call out your limitations. The reason to do this lies in the fact that keeping your head in the sand will not make shortcomings go away. If, for example, you admit that you hate to write and you tend to do anything to avoid it, you will be able to say something like, "…writing is a real pain for me, because I don't think I am very good at it. But this dissertation is VERY important to me, and I will suck it up and dive into my authoring…" As an aside, most published authors hate to write!!!

Note that items on your weakness list should include any habits/routines/imperfections that get in the way of working on your manuscript. These might include: the inability to focus for extended periods of time, the inability to plan effectively, the reluctance to set short-term goals, and an overall lack of confidence.

Identifying Your Opportunities

Opportunities offer a bright and shining star in the dissertation journey since they can be rooted in a hopeful future. "Oh the Places you'll go," from Dr. Seuss doesn't begin to describe the path ahead for a newly minted doctoral graduate. Taking stock of a positive future can keep you on track to completing your dissertation.

So take a look around and assess your current financial, professional, and personal environment. Think about how your finances might improve with a promotion at work or a new and financially more lucrative position. Will you ascend to the next echelon in your organization? Will you find a new profession and more meaningful work at a higher salary? Think also about your professional standing in your community. Will you be able to take on new responsibilities? Will you find a position that will more thoroughly utilize your new skill set? Additionally, think about how you will feel about yourself on a deeply personal level. Will you stand taller? Will you share your personal insights more freely with your family and friends? Will you become a lifelong learner?

All the above questions are worth asking and then answering for yourself in a very specific and individualized manner. Taking time to address your potential opportunities will further anchor your "WHY" of pursuing your doctorate and help keep you on course during the dissertation journey.

Identifying Your Threats

Perhaps nothing can derail the dissertation process faster than identified or unidentified threats. Not all surprises are good and the bad ones can be shocking. I like to advise my dissertation students to consider and keep a "Plan B" in their hip pocket. That is to say, a plan that addresses what you would do just in case things don't go according to plan. This is where you plan for the worst case and prepare for and mitigate it in advance of it occurring.

For example, a real threat for dissertation students is succumbing to the allure of buying a new computer while authoring their dissertation manuscript (more on this in Chapter 19). This is a threat with multiple dimensions. Consider the time it takes to fully transition to the new computer. Also, think about lost files, images, and software. I have yet to see a student migrate to a new computer without losing time, work, and patience! Be sure to have your Plan B ready if you choose to change computers. Have backup files prepared, use YouTube to familiarize yourself with the nuances of the computer in advance of purchasing it, and prepare to do a lot of deep breathing when your shiny new toy arrives!

The array of potential threats for a dissertation student can seem unending. Always remember to plan ahead as much as possible and keep those Plan B's ready for your unique circumstances!

Chapter 13

THE OUTLINE AND PROJECT PLAN

"I'm a big fan of outlining. Here's the theory: If I outline, then I can see the mistakes I'm liable to make. They come out more clearly in the outline than they do in the pages."
— Cynthia Voigt

There is no substitute for a well-architected dissertation outline – this is your roadmap. The time you spend creating your outline will save you countless hours writing your dissertation and has an added benefit of serving as your guide for your defense presentations. Your outline helps to support your dissertation project plan and provides structure and organization to your thoughts and ideas. It brings clarity and organization to your dissertation. It clarifies your main ideas and organizes them in a logical sequence. By outlining your main points and supporting details, you maintain focus on your topic, and you make sure your writing remains on track. One suggestion I like to offer my students is to start with a proposal defense that speaks to all that is important in their dissertations. It actually offers an outline of how to author the first three chapters of the dissertation! In addition to this, your outline allows you to plan and develop each section separately – and ultimately make the writing process less overwhelming. While compiling your outline, write a project plan (with actions, timelines, approval cycles, and concurrent activities) and stick to it like you have never stuck to anything before – you must be like a dog with a bone!

As an added benefit, having an outline gives you confidence in your writing by reducing writer's block and providing a clear framework. Perhaps, most importantly, an outline is a flexible tool and can be adjusted and revised as you progress in your writing. Please note, your outline is not set in stone! Your outline is a living document that you should plan to adjust as time and events demand. This is especially true of the dates you associate with your milestones. These will be edited (shorter or longer) as your dissertation journey evolves. All told, creating an outline that incorporates a project plan creates structure, organization, and enhances the overall quality of your work.

One process you might find helpful as you identify all the necessary steps in your dissertation journey, and maybe even surprising, is to create a two-way project timeline. This is a process where you use your outline to create a project plan and estimate the time it will take to develop your dissertation from beginning to end. Then, you create your time estimate by starting from the end of the project and going back to the beginning. This comparison will allow you to identify flaws in your estimate of completing the dissertation in a timely manner. The approach will allow you to stay on track. It will also allow you to make changes and see the temporal impact of those changes.

As a first step, create a traditional project plan starting with the present day and moving to the end date of a completed dissertation.

As a second step, begin with the end in mind and work backwards. Begin with the desired completion date and then estimate the days each step is going to take in reverse until you reach today. Have you completed all the necessary steps as you reached today? This is where most students realize that there are many time-consuming steps they generally don't think about. For example, including time for the IRB to complete its review and the iterations that may be involved for you to gain approval. In general, it's a good idea to plan for the IRB to take at least two weeks for each review iteration and to take one to three days for you to respond to these reviews with your revisions. One of the ways to ensure you are making progress is to establish indicators for measuring progress. All along your timeline, identify the most critical steps. This may be: completing the first draft of each chapter, submitting your IRB application, or interviewing and/or surveying your participants. Regardless of which indicators you choose, completing each one will build your confidence in achieving your goal of a published dissertation while keeping you on track. More often than not, the forward approach and the backward approach are not in alignment! You will find that you may be more optimistic when creating your forward plan and run out of time when using the backwards/ retrofitting approach. The bottom line is – set your goals, devise your game plan, and revise as necessary![39]

Chapter 14

THE JOURNAL

"Your journal will stand as a chronicle of your growth, your hopes, your fears, your dreams, your ambitions, your sorrows, your serendipities."

— Kathleen Adams

Many times, during your dissertation journey, you may think of other topics to weave into your manuscript. Be very careful – you may be approaching a "rabbit hole" zone here! You know these ideas are incredible for more research, and you may be tempted to increase the scope of your dissertation. Do not fall prey to this urge. Permitting "scope creep" will never get you to your goal of a completed manuscript. Instead, use a journal to capture your ideas for future article research (think of it as a parking lot). Simply put – stay the course!

Keeping a journal does not need to be time-consuming. Quick bullets will capture your thoughts and feelings. All told, your journal will preserve ideas and experiences during the dissertation expedition that you will want to review years from now. So take a few minutes each day, especially when you feel overwhelmed, and let your thoughts flow. Make your journal a judgment-free

113

zone and enjoy a process that will help you understand the full range of what you are experiencing, in what will probably be a once-in-a-lifetime process.

Your journal can also be quite helpful when you are feeling that your dissertation will never be completed and you are a lost cause. This is the time to go back and review what you have already written. In all likelihood, you have felt this way before! Revisiting the past and reflecting on how you were able to get beyond this hurdle will bring you comfort in the fact that your feeling of hopelessness is a temporary one and it will soon resolve itself. This is the time to take a walk and then come back to work on your dissertation.

In sum, over time, keeping a journal will help you see how much you grow as a person, how much your thoughts evolve, and give you alternative perspectives on your subject matter. Most importantly, you will develop a better understanding of you!

Chapter 15

THE INTENTIONS LOG

"The act of writing down your intentions solidifies your commitment to them, making it more likely that you'll follow through."
— *Unknown*

Intentionality can be wonderfully effective when it comes to achieving a goal. It is, in fact, instrumental in avoiding the stress and scrambling that occurs when you have procrastinated. Waiting until the last minute is something students are known for – but it's not because they are lazy; it is because they haven't come to terms with the concepts of time and urgency. When a milestone seems far away, we can decide to worry about it later and relegate it to something for our "future us." The longer away the due date is, the less urgency we assign to it, hence the more we procrastinate. Urgency only kicks in when the finish line comes into focus. In general, students are characterized as waiting until the night before an assignment is due to start working on it. Unfortunately, this does not work for dissertation writing! The more a doctoral student "rushes" a dissertation milestone, the more the product becomes an abysmal failure. This is the classic example of "you snooze, you lose!" This is where an intentions log can save the day. The following addresses the "how to" of your intentions log.

First off, create a spreadsheet for your week where you can keep tabs on your schedule and how much time you are devoting to your dissertation.[40] It's a great idea to actually schedule your dissertation time on your calendar (90 minutes is what I suggest). Your dissertation is important, and it deserves real estate on your calendar as much as any meeting or social event! This being said, know your personal best time of day – it doesn't matter when, it just matters that it is your best time! For many, it is early morning. I learned from a personal performance coach that getting up one to two hours before everyone else in your household gives you the freedom to attend to your most important project![41] This occurs because you have more quiet, more focus, and fewer distractions.

Second, an intentions log allows you to pat yourself on the back for what you accomplished during the last week and to set your intentions for the following week. I have found that people who use this log accomplish more, faster. I have also found that my dissertation students who used this log religiously reduced the timeline for writing their dissertations by a full year on average! I have included the template for the intentions log in Appendix D.

Please note that the intentions log is not a "to-do" list. It is a document that consistently captures key intended **results,** not simply action items. Yes, I said **results**. For example, your results do not include the number of peer-reviewed journal articles you read – results would include the articles that actually contribute to your literature review. Do not spend your precious time writing and including minutiae! For example, I have had students who included inconsequential information in their logs. They spoke to the phone calls they made, the emails they wrote, and non-academic books they perused! Instead, only include those actions that created **results** for your dissertation!

Chapter 16

THE REFERENCE LIBRARY AND LOCATING ADDITIONAL RESOURCES

"A library is a house of hope. It's a place where we all, whatever our situation, can feed our ideas and develop our dreams."
— Doug Wilhelm

Your dissertation reference library is the life-blood for citing and referencing information in your dissertation. In advance of "putting pen to paper," you should begin a thorough review of the literature for your topic. This is the time to build a spreadsheet library with potential sources for your dissertation. I personally spent three months researching a plethora of peer-reviewed journal articles and entering relevant information into a spreadsheet. Appendix F – Resource Template Sample is a plausible template you may want to use as you architect a topic-specific library for your resource information. In it, you will include a column to identify the types of information included in each article you have chosen for possible inclusion in your literature review. Simply use identifiers that can be quite helpful and allow you to sort and see that you have multiple sources addressing a given area. Your spreadsheet is your reference library – and it is your friend – use it every day as you build one incredible lit review and sources for other areas of your dissertation! As an aside, this spreadsheet is a useful place to store quotations you may want for future reference.

One masterful way to add to your reference library is to identify an article you find useful, then check out the references listed at the end of that article. It's amazing how many additional quality references are there for you to include while expanding your research. One note of warning – when looking for reference material for your dissertation – stay away from low-end references! Use only peer-reviewed journal articles, well-regarded conference proceedings, and books from highly regarded authors and researchers in your field.

Part V

WARNINGS!

Chapter 17

YOU KNOW WHAT THEY SAY ABOUT ASSUMPTIONS!

"Assumptions are the windows on the world. Scrub them off every once in a while, or the light won't come in."

— *Isaac Asimov*

One of the biggest mistakes students make about their dissertation timeline is overlooking the time required by others involved in their dissertation journey. Too often, students **assume** their chair, IRB reviewer, etc. sit like "Maytag Repairmen" waiting for students to send them documents for review. Students oftentimes expect others to work nights and weekends to expedite review cycles! So, don't assume your chair, committee members, or others will review your files and drafts in real time. Common courtesy suggests allowing a two-week timeframe for manuscript reviews.

In addition, also keep in mind that your study participants will not respond in real-time. Also, the IRB can cost you from weeks to months to complete your review, especially when there is a need for additional information about your participant pool if it is a group that may be in danger from your research protocol. Even though I had a straight-forward methodology in my dissertation that would not present a risk to my participants, it still took the IRB 84 days to respond with approval!

And on a final note regarding delays, keep in mind that it takes time to have your defenses scheduled, as well as a period of time for final clearance of your dissertation. This brings me to a very important word, "Wait." Oftentimes students tell me they are waiting for something: the IRB review, manuscript review, scheduling times for their defenses, etc. This is so wrong on many levels. The fact is that these are the times students should be working on other tasks. For example, while you "wait" for your chair to review your proposal, begin creating your PPT for your proposal defense. Simply because you are in a "wait" state does not mean that you should be sitting on your hands! The fact is that "Wait" is a bad four-letter word. Along the lines of planning for others to take time for their reviews, at no time during your dissertation journey should you use the excuse "I'm waiting for…" For example, "I'm waiting for the IRB to get back to me," "I'm waiting for my chair to finish her review," "I'm waiting for the school to schedule my proposal defense!" Though you may be inclined to say you are waiting for reviews and approvals, this is not when you should shut down! Consider using this time to prepare the slide deck for your proposal defense, or to begin writing your IRB application. Yes, you may need to make edits based on the results of your defense, but if you have done a good job and have a dissertation chair who has given you valuable guidance while you were writing the proposal, your edits should be minimal.

Simply put, you need to bolster your timeline and not assume that others will turn things around for you at the drop of a hat. As you build your dissertation timeline – begin with the end in mind and allocate appropriate periods of time for each stage of the process!

Chapter 18

NO NEW COMPUTERS DURING DISSERTATION!

"Buying a new computer is a lot like a blind date. You hope for the best but expect the worst."

— Unknown

As tempting as it may be, refrain from buying a new computer during dissertation. "New and Improved" doesn't mean that your transition process will go smoothly. Usually, you will be left coming to grips with new technology, misplaced files, and configuration management issues!

All told, there are several reasons why you should not buy a new computer while you are writing your dissertation. First of all, purchasing a new computer during the dissertation writing process can introduce unnecessary disruptions and distractions. You are already familiar and comfortable using your current computer system. This is an advantage since you are accustomed to its operating system, software, and settings. If you "upgrade" to a new computer, especially with different configurations and software, you will need to invest additional time and effort to set up and become comfortable with the new environment. This transition period will

125

divert attention away from the crucial task of dissertation writing and leave you feeling frustrated and overwhelmed!

Next, compatibility issues come into play. Software licenses, data files, and customized settings specific to the old computer may not seamlessly transfer to the new system. This can result in compatibility issues or even data loss. And don't forget the time and effort required to transfer files and adapt to new software versions; these can seriously disrupt your dissertation writing process as well as your focus and introduce errors or inconsistencies in your work.

Moreover, the availability of technical support and familiarity with one's current computer system can be advantageous. Over time, users become accustomed to troubleshooting common issues and navigating the quirks of their existing computer. They may have identified workarounds or developed strategies to optimize performance, saving valuable time during the dissertation writing process. With a new computer, you will likely encounter unfamiliar problems or require technical assistance, potentially causing more delays or frustration.

The crucial question you need to ask yourself here is, "do I really need a new system?" In most (if not all) cases, your current computer may already possess the necessary capabilities to handle the demands of your academic writing, research, and data analysis. Unless there are requirements that cannot be met by your current system, investing in a new computer may be an unnecessary financial and temporal expense.

Finally, consider the time you will spend just researching, selecting, and setting up a new computer. This time could be better allocated towards writing, conducting research, and refining your dissertation.

By avoiding the distraction of acquiring a new computer, you can keep your "eye on the prize" of completing your dissertation.

In sum, though a new computer may be calling to you, you must consider the disruptions, compatibility issues, and time issues associated with such a purchase. It is essential to consider if the benefits of a new computer outweigh the setbacks during your critical dissertation writing process.

Chapter 19

LIFE HAPPENS – STRIKE WHILE THE IRON IS HOT!

"Life is what happens when you're busy making other plans."
— *Allen Saunders*

When you began your dissertation journey you did so with the belief that you could achieve your goal of donning graduation regalia, walking the stage, and being called "Dr.!" You were optimistic that if you invested effort each day, you would complete your magnum opus in record time and with stellar results.

And then life happened! You weren't counting on family emergencies with parents and children. You weren't counting on losing your job and needing to spend countless hours trying to find another one. You weren't counting on getting COVID. The list goes on and on and robs you of countless hours that you could have been working on your dissertation.

This is where consistency comes into play. The fact is that consistency matters. It will get you through the tough times. All told, consistency provides a solid foundation for growth, progress, and achievement. By embracing consistency in your dissertation actions, behaviors, and commitments, you set yourself up for long-term success and achievement of this very important goal. This is where "come hell or high water," you maintain your dissertation efforts. Remember, you are only contributing 90 minutes per day to your dissertation, so stick with it! Consider the story of the compounding penny. Double a penny for 30 days and you will have over $5 million. But double a penny every other day for 30 days and you will only have just over $300! With your dissertation, consistency means steady progress where you develop and achieve noticeable advancements in a shorter time. Keep in mind that every time you start and then stop work on your dissertation, you lose both your momentum and your train of thought.

By remaining consistent in the dissertation process, you strengthen your discipline and self-control muscles! So, how do you develop this consistency muscle in your dissertation, and why specifically does it matter? Consider trying the following.

Define a positive habit for your dissertation journey and then practice it repeatedly until it becomes rooted and virtually effortless. For example, schedule a specific time each day to work on your dissertation. As this becomes a consistent habit, you will find that your dissertation begins to mature into an impressive manuscript. Remember, habits need to be repeated to become consistent and second nature.

The long-term success of your dissertation demands consistency! Consistency is a crucial factor for completing and achieving long-term success. Consistency is what enables you to maintain momentum, overcome obstacles, and sustain positive habits and behaviors that contribute to sustained success in the dissertation process. If you are inconsistent with your research approach, you will likely end up with a dissertation that lacks cohesiveness and, worse yet, offers no answers to your research questions! For example, painstakingly and consistently researching each subtopic of your dissertation in your literature review will help expose the gaps in the literature that establish the need for you to further research your topic.

Consistency on your part promotes personal and professional growth. For example, by consistently engaging in activities that nurture your physical, mental, and emotional well-being, such as exercise, meditation, or journaling, you can enhance your overall quality of life and set the stage for successfully accomplishing your dissertation goals. In addition, by consistently investing time and effort into your professional development, such as the continuous learning and skill-building that accompanies your doctoral journey, you increase your dissertation expertise, expand your research opportunities, and advance your academic standing.

Consistency is crucial for achieving a completed and approved dissertation. For example, by consistently taking small steps towards your dissertation, you stay on track and increase the likelihood of completing your magnum opus. It is the discipline and self-control that comes with consistency, strengthens your willpower, enhances your focus, and leads you to your ultimate dissertation goal.

And finally, oddly enough, consistency serves to improve your efficiency and effectiveness. By following consistent processes, you develop approaches to working on your dissertation that will save you time, reduce errors, and increase your productivity. Since consistency actually aids in learning and retention, you can learn and reinforce what you have learned over time, enhance memory retention, and create a learning process that is more efficient and effective.

Even though there is no way, short of being a fortune teller, that you can predict when life will happen. The best you can do is to employ these two ideas. First of all, as you prepare your project timeline, include buffers for unexpected events and stay the course consistently. In other words, instead of planning an unrealistically demanding dissertation schedule, ramp it down a bit to allow for emergencies and for personal time! Secondly, anytime you find an unscheduled slice of time, leverage it to your advantage and "invest" it in your dissertation. Consistent efforts coupled with realistic timeline goals will win the day!

Chapter 20

YOU WILL NEED A BOUNCE HOUSE!

"When the road gets bumpy, make sure you've got your bounce house ready to roll."

— *Unknown*

Remember when you were able to focus on and dissect many ideas at the same time? What happened to that person? That person is writing a dissertation! While you are in the midst of authoring your manuscript, you will find you are consistently thinking about it and losing track of other important areas of your life. You no longer seem able to disengage from your dissertation and reengage with work projects, friends, and family to the same degree as before you began this huge doctoral endeavor.

Rough waters don't begin to describe the average dissertation journey! Just as in the open seas, clouds will gather, the wind will pick up, and storms will come. Whether it's in the form of self-imposed perfectionism, negative input from your chair, or worse yet a lost manuscript file, you will face challenges that leave you feeling that all is lost and that this goal can never be achieved. Not to worry, this is completely normal!

Becoming resilient and practicing a few basics will help you build a "bounce house" for yourself and alleviate the challenges and the feelings that come with them. Begin by simply admitting how you are feeling! All too often we dismiss our sensitivities, sometimes because we were raised to stuff our feelings, dismiss our feelings, and even eat our feelings! We may tell ourselves that what happened and what we are experiencing is no big deal. Worse yet, our friends and family may dismiss what we are experiencing and condescendingly tell us that we are overreacting and instead of "freaking out", we should just "chill"!

So this is a good time to be realistic about what may be causing you to overreact to input and criticism. Are you a perfectionist? Are you being overly self-critical? This is the time to ask yourself, *"Is my perfectionism getting in the way of getting things done?"* You may need a bounce house!

Without fail, I work with dissertation students who remain in edit mode for what seems like forever! They write and rewrite the same paragraphs and sections countless times! I remember working with one student who spent a year revising her Chapter 1! As you might have guessed, she never finished her dissertation and wears the "scarlet letters" ABD. Whether you are authoring a dissertation, a journal article, or a book – keep writing. There is a time for editing, but not during the authoring process. Get your first draft written as a brain dump. This permits you to address the most important aspects of your work early on.

The phrase, perfect is the enemy of good, speaks to how you can get caught up in making things perfect and, unfortunately, never really getting anything done. The phrase comes from the French proverb *"l'ennemi du bien est le bien"* and is attributed to

Voltaire. It is translated to "The best is the enemy of the good." Moving quickly and growing often means risking failure. You can't make everyone love your work. For the most part, done is better than perfect! So take the stance that sometimes, simple and done is far better than perfect and unfinished.

What this means is that people who are striving for perfection are actually their own worst enemy. They're so busy trying to make everything perfect, looking for the best, they don't notice when progress will make a bigger difference than perfection.

Also, it is important to keep in mind that perfectionism can have a strong negative effect on your mental health. It can lead you to literally quit your doctoral journey when you believe you can't get things right. This is the time to forget "all-or-nothing thinking."[42] Try to keep in mind that the opposite of perfection isn't failure. It's simply a willingness to take risks and thrive in the ambiguity of not knowing if your work product is good enough.

What all this boils down to is that for a dissertation student, the drive for perfection leads to an overly lengthy and unhealthy process. It is important to remember that most, if not all universities, have a time limit on completing a doctoral program which includes approval of the final dissertation manuscript and defense thereof. In addition to university-imposed time limits, you can run into a situation where your citations/references and research become dated and necessitate that you perform additional research to ensure a contemporary research approach. Nobody wants to start over! Don't let yourself lose all your hard work because you have run out of time! And don't let your research become so old that it no longer has merit!

There is an adage that states, "You can't steer a parked car." There's nothing wrong with striving to do a good job – but you must realize the ramifications. Perfection isn't an end in itself – it is not the be all and end all. It is how you view your dissertation in order to identify areas for improvement. Oftentimes, what really paralyzes us is the fear of failure.[43] Do not let this be you – you are perfectly capable of researching and creating an outstanding dissertation, or you would not have gotten this far! Believe in yourself and your intellectual prowess!

Something that often comes as a surprise to dissertation students is that the desire for perfection can actually prevent excellent work. Striving for progress rather than perfection allows you the space to try and learn to produce excellent work! In tech, this concept has become something of a battle cry. Business startups depend on innovation to address the white space in growing markets where they focus on the minimum acceptable product. Such business leaders encourage their employees to let go of the idea of perfection and focus instead on getting things done. The intent is to create ideas and take risks.[44] Let this be your focus as well!

On another level, acknowledging your sensitivities and admitting to your feelings of disappointment, sadness, or embarrassment can bring you to the point where you can reframe the situation. For example, rather than telling yourself that your dissertation chair lambasted you for how you wrote your Chapter 3, reframe the criticism to translate her harsh words into a framework of helping you turn your manuscript into the best it could be. Another way to look at it is to redefine your thoughts of "She criticized my work because she doesn't like me" into "I'm so disappointed she criticized my work – I need to take action and do some rewriting. After all, every great author needs to edit and rewrite!" This important first step shifts the responsibility to you; not to what you believe the other person thinks of you.

Now for the fun part! The next time you notice a judgmental tone creeping into your thoughts, have some compassion for yourself. Reframe the way you talk to yourself to one where you translate your thoughts into the way you would counsel a friend. If a friend told you they were incompetent, would you agree with them? No, you would not! Instead, you would say that they are smart and fully competent. So too, be a friend to yourself and reinforce your own confidence and well-being. *Bottom line, squash your inner-critic!*

Finally, ask yourself what is the lesson-learned from this situation? This is where "perceived failures" become "opportunities to learn and improve." This is the one approach that works best for me because it gives me hope and the knowledge that I will do better the next time around.

All told, people who are resilient are able to recover quickly from difficult situations and tend to view rejection or disappointment as an opportunity to learn about themselves and grow. They frequently say "next time…" This is also true for you and your dissertation journey. If you lose an important file for your manuscript, look at how you manage your files. Do you keep all of your important files in only one location? Set up a backup configuration that saves your files to the cloud, a backup drive, etc. Let this action be your "next time" bounce house to resilience!

Part VI

THE BEST IS YET TO COME!

Chapter 21

EVERY DISSERTATION DESERVES A BOOK!

"A dissertation is the foundation, but a book is the legacy. Take pride in the process of turning your scholarly work into a timeless contribution to your field."

— *Unknown*

At this point you must be thinking, seriously? Here you are, feeling that you may never complete your manuscript, and here I am telling you to write a book that is a derivative of your dissertation! I am here to encourage you to envision the book that will follow your dissertation. I would like you to dream of what the book would look like. How many pages do you see? What will your cover look like? How will it feel at your book launch, signing copies of what you believe is the greatest tome ever? Create that image in your mind and see it every time the going gets rough, whenever you are frustrated by your dissertation chair, and any time you are too tired to write another word.

One of the best things about turning your dissertation into a book is that people will actually read it! When you create your dissertation, it is basically read only by your dissertation committee.

After it is published in ProQuest (yes, they own the rights!), perhaps a handful of other researchers will do a quick read. However, when you author your book, your dissertation takes on a new life. Though you will need to rewrite the dissertation due to publisher rights, you will want to revise your dissertation to make for enjoyable reading. In its current state, the dissertation is written in "academic-ese" and is not an enticing read. Rewriting the dissertation takes the manuscript to a new and read-worthy level. This is where your unique voice comes through and where you can weave in your own sense of humor, and sometimes sarcasm!

On a personal note, I was driven to translate my dissertation into a book *"The Invisible Leader"* because I was disappointed (like many of my colleagues) to realize that other than my dissertation committee, very few people would ever read my "labor of love." So when I rewrote the dissertation, I folded in personal stories (yes, bias is permitted in your stories). This gave my book a more interesting tone and gave readers a chance to see themselves in my predicaments. I was also able to align my chapters to include take-away thoughts and ideas for implementing what they had learned.

If you are a business-person or an entrepreneur, authoring a book from what you have compiled in your dissertation can open doors to increased opportunities. Please know that in this day and age, a book creates credibility and authenticity for the author – it has, in fact, virtually replaced the business card! When you carry the moniker Doctor and you have a book that showcases your knowledge and knowhow, doors open for you along with increased respect and the belief that you can create solutions for potential clients. Please don't ignore the opportunity to facilitate your rise to "Dr. Famous" by authoring your derivative dissertation in a book.

Chapter 22

A Growth Mindset Will Set You Up for Success

"The mind is just like a muscle – the more you exercise it, the stronger it gets and the more it can expand."

— Idowu Koyenikan

Your growth mindset includes your ability to see challenges and mistakes as opportunities. You are working on your dissertation; that, in and of itself, is an indicator of your growth mindset. So don't let fears and perturbations get in your way! Your love for learning is your best tool for maintaining this growth mindset and plowing your way through the dissertation sojourn.

It is said that we are most influenced by the five people with whom we spend the greatest amount of time. Including naysayers in this special group will do nothing to further your quest of completing your doctoral dissertation. In fact, these people may derail your efforts and leave you in the dust of ABD! Be sure to surround yourself with a tribe of growth-oriented members as they will encourage your progress, enable your resilience, and help you steer from an "I can't" attitude to an "I got this" way of thinking.

In research conducted by Stanford University psychologist Carol Dweck, survey participants were asked if they believed,

"You have a certain amount of intelligence, and you can't really do much to change it." The way they answered this indicated whether they leaned towards a "growth mindset" or a "fixed mindset." For those who thought there wasn't much they could do to change their intelligence, they were characterized as people with a fixed mind set. However, those who believed they could affect a change in their lives, were said to have a growth mindset and thrive on inspiration from others.[45] The research revealed that teachers, coaches, and managers are integral to influencing our growth mindset. This is yet another reason to choose a dissertation chair who is positive, inspiring, and motivating. When you think you are not able to write another word, your chair can be your best coach and cheerleader to get you over this rough spot.

In another experiment, the brains of people who have growth mindsets were compared with those who have fixed mind-sets through the use of trivia tests. The brain images of the participants showed that after missing a question, those with a growth mindset were more attentive to the correct answer. While those with fixed mindsets were less interested in learning the right answer and instead showed an emotional response to getting the question wrong.[46] This type of emotional response can keep you from developing a growth mind-set. I like to think of the fixed mind-set as the character "Eeyore," a fictional character developed by A.A. Milne. Eeyore can best be described as negative and pessimistic. He practices victim-speak and rarely, if ever, finds the good in a situation. On the other hand, Winnie-the-Pooh is the persona who is optimistic and consistently tries his best. While these two characters are friends and able to influence the thinking of one another, they teach us the value of positivism, growth, and learning.

And even though it is easy for us to assess the mindset of each character, it is a challenge for most of us to see ourselves as being fixed in a negative and victim mindset.

"People start thinking that having a growth mindset makes you a better all-around human being, and no one wants to fess up to being 'fixed,'" said Susan Mackie, co-founder of the Growth Mindset Institute in Melbourne, Australia. "It meant that people started to feel they should hide their fixed mindsets. Instead, people start saying, 'I have a growth mindset.' Simply saying you have a growth mindset does not always mean you have one." For you, as a dissertation student, it is difficult to maintain a growth orientation when the dissertation process is so challenging and imposing on your life.

For you, a true growth mindset will involve trying new strategies and seeking help when you are stuck. One of the best strategies is to actually acknowledge that you are sinking into a fixed mindset, i.e. catch yourself when you find yourself using negative self-talk. This is the time to say "stop" out loud, congratulate yourself, and continue researching! In addition, certain triggers can help you move from a fixed to a growth mindset. For example, praise yourself for a specific dissertation milestone, like the completion of your literature review. I like to use the "that was easy" button – in fact, I keep it on my desk next to me while I work! You can also use self-talk like "…I know this dissertation is going to be challenging, but I am smart, I am prepared, and I have the resources to get the job done…I have a growth mindset with a desire to research and learn!" And speaking of quotations, look to Appendix F (Quotations to Motivate You During Your Dissertation Journey) if you are ever in need of some extra words to guide and inspire your growth mindset!

Chapter 23

THE SURPRISES ALONG THE WAY

"In the midst of chaos, there is also opportunity."
—*Sun Tzu*

At the end of their dissertation journeys, many of my students shared the surprises they encountered along the way. Here are some of the more interesting ones. These include, in the realm of qualitative research, the overall interview process resulted in hundreds of transcribed pages of information. While much of the time their participants remained on topic, quite a few went off on tangents, filling pages of the interview document with irrelevant information. Some participants were likened to asking someone for the time and them answering by how to build a watch! Quite frequently, the interviews went on well beyond the anticipated time. It is generally not advised that students abort the interview when the prescribed time has been reached. Hence, the students end up with hundreds of pages of transcribed material.

Other participants offered "surprise" responses that, at times, were epiphanies to the researcher. For example, one student learned from one of her participants that the leader of his organization created a hostile work environment by belittling employees and calling them names like "fat," "unattractive," and "stupid." This is clearly not the situation where the interviewer would divulge the identity of the participant since these interviews are confidential by form. However, the harsh and abusive leadership style was certainly included in the final dissertation without attribution.

For the most part, participants are quite insightful and were able to provide responses that were deep and meaningful. These are the participants who set the stage for follow-on questions, where such questions created the path to defining categories and themes.

One unfortunate surprise occurred when students lost files or inadvertently deleted their manuscripts (without backup files!). This often took place when students were replacing an older computer with a new one. Being organized and employing a file configuration management system quickly became the obvious solution to losing or misplacing files.

Yet another unfortunate surprise occurred when a student was unable to gain access to research participants. While most students' approach to acquiring participants seems to make sense in the proposal stage, many students find that their perceived "gold mine" of participants does not exist. It is important to keep in mind that as you apply filters to your sample population, you reduce the number of possible participants. For example, if you are only interested in participants who are male, from 30 to 45 years old, single, working in a managerial position, employed in the IT field for at least five years, residing in San Diego, having a Master's Degree in Mathematics, and working specifically in the area of generative AI, your potential sample is far smaller than if you did not employ so many filters. Hence, it may come as a surprise if you find that you cannot obtain an adequate sample size for your research. This is especially true if you are doing quantitative research, where the requirement for the number of participants is significantly larger than for qualitative research.

Finally, one surprise that caught a dissertation student was about her own self-concept. What she came to discover was that she was dragging her feet with her dissertation since she was afraid of the future. She was afraid she would not be able to find a job following graduation; she was doubtful that her friends and family would criticize her for not landing a high salaried position; and she was worried that she would not be deemed smart enough to have earned a doctorate.

As you complete your dissertation journey, I'm sure you will encounter surprises of your own. Just remember to take them in stride and pat yourself on the back for every victory along the way. The day will come when you look back on the experience with incredible fondness for your talents, your professors, your cohort friends, and your chair!

Chapter 24

THE FINALE TO YOUR TERMINAL DEGREE!

"An end is only a beginning in disguise."
— *Craig D. lounsbrough*

It's finally here. It's graduation day, and you have earned the right to celebrate – big time! Make no mistake, the process was grueling, and you deserve all the pampering, gifts, and self-love you can handle. Protect these celebratory moments and ignore all the questions you get about "what's next?" For example, friends and family will ask, "when will you be getting that big job with the even bigger paycheck?" But probably the worst question you may hear on graduation day is "what did this piece of paper cost you (or your family)?" Ignore all the pushy, rude, and jealous comments and questions! You can think about all those questions about future plans and paying back student loans after you have savored the ecstasy of your incredible accomplishment.

Speaking of money, soon after graduation day, spare no expense and order a very large and expensive frame for your glorious diploma. I know a number of doctoral candidates who even order their diploma frames a year in advance of the big day. Some candidates even purchase graduation regalia as much as two years in advance of graduating!

As a final word about completing your doctorate, and this will take some time, but you will also need to get used to being called "Doctor." Sometimes, you may find yourself turning around to see who is being called doctor! You will need to get to use the title doctor, but as they say at Toyota, "Oh what a feeling!!!"

Appendices

GENERAL DISSERTATION CHAPTER CONTENTS

Section in the Dissertation
CHAPTER 1: INTRODUCTION TO THE STUDY [47, 48, 49, 50]
1. The Introduction to the Study Section: You need to have a clear statement demonstrating that the focus of the study is on a significant issue or problem worthy of study. Be sure to include a brief, well-articulated summary of the relevant research literature that substantiates a need for studying the issue or problem. If there is no need, why are you doing the study?
2. The Problem Statement: This is where you describe the issue or problem to be studied. Be sure to include a purpose statement clearly articulating the specific objectives of your research.
3. The Theoretical Orientation or Conceptual Framework: This is where you delineate the ideas or concepts you are applying to the issue or problem under investigation. Your narrative provides descriptions of the ideas or concepts and their relevance to the issue or problem you have chosen to research – it briefly links the descriptions to prior knowledge and research.
4. The Research Questions: You need to clearly state your research questions. Be sure your research questions are directly connected to the theoretical orientation or conceptual framework.
5. Operational Definitions: In this section, you will define the technical terms and special word uses of your research.

6. The Significance of the Study:
This section is where you provide a rationale for your study. This can be described in terms of:

> Application to educational leadership,
> Generation or extension of knowledge,
> Implications for social or organizational change, or
> Advancement of a methodological approach for examining the issue or problem under study.

7. Summary of the key points of the chapter:
Chapter 1 ends with a synopsis of major sections and concepts that were reviewed, and an overview of the contents of the remaining chapters in the dissertation.

Section in the Dissertation

CHAPTER TWO: REVIEW OF THE RELATED LITERATURE [51, 52, 53, 54]

1. The Introduction to the chapter:
This is where you provide a re-statement of the purpose of the study. This section also includes an overall summary of the content of the literature review to come. Be sure to describe how your literature review is organized.

2. The body of literature review:
Your literature review is not merely a bibliography – it is integrated to the extent that it offers comparisons and contrasts of your sources and includes comparisons of different points of view or different research outcomes. Be sure to organize this chapter around major ideas or themes. In this chapter, you will need to make explicit connections between prior knowledge and research and the issue or problem under investigation. Be sure to explain the connection of all referenced studies or thematic areas to the proposed study and present a full explanation of the theoretical orientation or conceptual framework.
Your narrative should include:
Concise summaries of literature that help substantiate the rationale for the theoretical orientation or conceptual framework, as well as a rationale for its selection.

3. The contents of the review is drawn from:
The most relevant published knowledge and current research on the topic under investigation. Scholarly sources, such as books, peer-reviewed journals, or other materials appropriate to the issue or problem chosen for study.

> **4.** The contents of your review may also include a **review of literature related to the research design**, if not presented in Chapter 3.

> **5.** The chapter ends with a **Summary** of the literature review and its connection to the issue or problem you are investigating.

Section in the Dissertation

CHAPTER THREE: RESEARCH DESIGN [55, 56, 57, 58]

1. The Introduction includes a clear outline of the major areas of the chapter.

2. The Research Design derives logically from the problem statement and the purpose of the study. This is where you –
Include an explicit description of the design and methods.
Provide a justification for using the design and methods.
Offer an explanation of the steps taken to ensure the validity and reliability of the design (e.g., member checks, peer-debriefing, methodological triangulation).
Refer, as appropriate, to evidence of quality contained in the appendixes (e.g., sample transcripts, researcher logs, field notes).

3. The Population and Sample. This is where you ensure the Population and Sample are suitable for the study's purpose. This is where you –
Describe the population from which the sample is drawn.
Describe and defend the sampling method.
Describe and defend the sample size.
Describe the eligibility criteria for study participants (aka filters).

4. The Instruments and data collection tools. This is where you –
Ensure these are consistent with the research approach and the theoretical orientation or conceptual framework.
This is where you –
Present descriptions of each instrument or data collection tool (e.g., interview guide).
    Name of instrument,
    Type of instrument,
    Concepts measured by instrument,
How the scores are derived and their meaning,
Include the processes for assessment of the reliability and validity of the instrument
Include a detailed description of data sources, the items, and their connection to the theoretical orientation or conceptual framework (i.e., Data Source Chart).

5. If a treatment is used, it is described clearly and in full detail.

6. The Data Collection. This is where you include –
The detailed description of procedures for recruiting study participants and collecting data. The study protocol that outlines the chronology of events for the conduct of the study. The statements about where raw data are or will be available (e.g., appendices, tables, or by request from the researcher).

7. The Data Analysis procedures. This is where you –
Confirm the research approach (quantitative, qualitative, or mixed methods). Ensure research–
> Is appropriate for the methods and instruments or tools.
> Is traceable to the purpose of the study, the research questions, and the methodology.

Includes –
> A precise description of the data analysis procedures.
> A description of the systems for keeping track of data and emerging understandings (research logs, reflective journals, cataloging systems).

8. The Protection of Human Subjects section provides a detailed description of the ethical measures taken for the protection of human subjects. **This is where you include –**
The processes for seeking participants' informed consent or, in the case of minors, their assent and the consent of parents or guardians.
The safeguards to maintain the confidentiality or anonymity of participants' private information, responses, or behavior, including the security of all raw data in any form.
The strategies for maintaining the confidentiality of information.
The voluntary nature of participation and that withdrawal will involve no penalty or loss of benefits to which participants are otherwise entitled.
The benefits for participation, if any (e.g., gift, money, experimental credits).
The foreseeable risks or discomforts.

9. The Limitations of the Study describe, where appropriate:
Facts assumed to be true but not actually verified.
Potential weaknesses of the study.
Boundaries of the study.
Researcher bias and how the research design controls for that bias.

Section in the Dissertation
CHAPTER FOUR: FINDINGS [59, 60, 61, 62]
1. The Introduction contains a clear, brief description of the processes that were used to gather and analyze data.
2. The research site and characteristics of the study participants.
3. The Findings (i.e., patterns, relationships, or themes). This is where you –   Build logically from the problem and purpose statements and the research questions.   Are supported by the data.
4. The Findings are presented and explained in a manner that: **Addresses each research question.**   Is consistent with the research approach (quantitative, qualitative, or mixed methods).   Is consistent with the theoretical orientation or conceptual framework.
5. Discrepant cases and non-confirming data are included, where appropriate.
6. The Tables and Figures used to present and organize data: Are as self-descriptive as possible.   Are referred to and commented on in the narrative.   Are properly identified (titled or captioned).   Show copyright permission if not in the public domain.
7. The chapter ends with a summary of the significant or most salient findings.

Section in the Dissertation
CHAPTER FIVE: CONCLUSIONS AND RECOMMENDATIONS [63, 64, 65, 66]
1. The chapter begins with a summary of the study (Chapters 1 - 4) - This is where you address -   The issue or problem under investigation and the purpose of the study.   The questions being addressed.   The theoretical orientation or conceptual framework that guided the study.   How the study was conducted.   The findings.

2. The Conclusions. This is where you –
Address the research questions and how they were answered.
Are bounded by the evidence collected and derived from the findings.
Include specific connections to the findings.
Establish the conclusion to a larger body of literature on the topic.
Transition to recommendations.

3. The Recommendations are implied by and logically connected to the conclusions.
They may address practice, leadership, policy, and social change or organizational
change. The narrative contains a full explanation for the recommendation:
Contains steps to useful action where appropriate.
Suggests to whom and how results might be disseminated.

4. The Recommendations for Future Research section. **This is where you –**
Present topics that need closer examination as suggested by the study findings.
Propose other methodologies that may be used to examine the issues related to the
study.

5. The work concludes with your thoughts about the implications of study.

RESEARCH DESIGNS[67]

The Selection of a Research Design

Qualitative (open-ended questions) late 20th century, quantitative, and mixed methods comprise the types of research designs.

Qualitative is the means for exploring and understanding the meaning we give to a social or human problem – honors an inductive style.

Quantitative is the means for testing objective theories by examining the relationships among variables.

Philosophical Worldviews – the basic set of beliefs that guide action –

1. postpositive – traditional, quantitative, scientific – cause and effect – reductionistic (reducing things to a discrete set of ideas).

2. social construction – approach to qualitative research – seeking understanding of the world – open-ended questions via interaction.

3. advocacy/participatory – holds that research inquiry needs to be intertwined with politics. and a political agenda – brings

focus to needs of the marginalized or disenfranchised – emancipatory.
4. pragmatic – mixed and multiple methods approach – different assumptions.

Strategies of Inquiry

Quantitative – cross-sections, longitudinal, experimental.

Qualitative –

1. narrative (studies the lives of 1 or 2 via interview and retells the story.
2. ethnographic (studies a cultural group in a natural setting via observation and interview).
3. grounded (participant views, multiple stages of data collection with emerging categories).
4. case studies (explores a program event, activity process – bounded by time and activity); phenomenological identifies the essence of human experiences as described by a few participants and prolonged engagement).

Mixed methods – sequential, concurrent with merging data, transformative.

Research Methods – the choice comes down to whether you want to specify the info to be collected or leave the questions open-ended.

Approach is driven by the experience of the researcher, the audience for whom the final report is being written, and the research problem,

Design = Worldview + research + strategies

Qualitative Procedures

These procedures define and describe the research design, the researcher's role, the site, participants, events, processes, ethics, data collection procedures, data analysis procedures, verification (via triangulation, member checking, repeated observations, peer examinations), clarification of researcher bias, and reporting.

Characteristics of qualitative research:

1. Natural setting,
2. researcher is key,
3. multiple sources,
4. inductive analysis (bottom up),
5. incorporating participant's meaning,
6. emergent design (as data becomes available),
7. theoretical lens like culture, gender, class etc.,
8. interpretive – based on what is seen,
9. holistic account – merges multiple perspectives,

Strategies of inquiry include data collection, coding and analysis, and writing.

The researcher's role – include past experiences, comments on connections with the participants, steps with the IRB, describe gaining entry to the setting, comments on sensitive issues – be specific and stretch your imagination about possibilities.

Data collection procedures – include the background to the purposeful selection of the participants and sites; provide a list of the types of data; observations (may be intrusive); interviews (presence may cause bias), documents (may be incomplete), audio/visual (may be disruptive).

Data recording procedures – define an observational protocol

1. Data analysis and interpretation – requires continual reflection, open-ended questions, 4-5 themes, steps include:
   - Organize and prepare the data
   - Read all the data

Begin the analysis with a coding process

[before proceeding, get a sense of the whole, review the most interesting doc, make a list of topics, assemble the data, recode if necessary].

Code the topics

Identify the codes that are surprising or unusual (process codes, activity codes, strategy codes, and relationship codes).

There is a plethora of software platforms to handle qualitative data that:

1. Use the coding process to generate the description of the setting/participants.
2. Describe how the themes will be represented.
3. Interpret – what lessons were learned.

Reliability, validity, and generalizability

Reliability

1. Check the transcripts for possible mistakes.

2. Look for "drift" away from the themes.
3. Coordinate communication among coders.
4. Cross check the codes.

Validity

1. Triangulate data sources.
2. Member checking.
3. Rich description.
4. Clarify bias.
5. Present info that runs counter.
6. Spend lots of time in the field.
7. Use peer debriefing.
8. Use and external auditor.

Generalizability

1. Quotes.
2. Script conversation.
3. Tables of info.
4. Wording that generates codes.
5. Narrative outcome described.

MILESTONE PROJECT MANAGEMENT CHART

Below is a general timeline example for keeping tabs on your dissertation progress at the macro level. This chart can help keep you on track especially if you have distractions that drag you away from your important goal of completing your manuscript!

TASK	START DATE	DURATION	END DATE	SPECIAL CIRCUMSTANCES AND DEPENDANCY NOTES
Identify your research topic.		1 week	1/8/24	Availability of your research chair to advise and concur in the topic.
Articulate the title (be specific and ensure your area of research is not too broad).		1 day	1/9/24	Approval of your dissertation chair.
Author Chapter 2 Perform a review of the literature ensuring there is a gap in that research that you need to address.		8 weeks		Personal time availability and review of draft chapter by your chair.
Author Chapter 1 – The Introduction.		4 weeks		Personal time availability and approval of your chair to move to this chapter.

Author Chapter 3 – Methodology.		4 weeks		Personal time availability and approval of your chair to move to this chapter.
Edit the chapters for approval to defend the Proposal.		3 weeks		Approval of chair to defend.
Send the Proposal to Chair.		1 day		
Chair's Review of Proposal.		2 weeks		
Send the Proposal to Committee with Chair's approval.		1 Day		
Committee Review prior to Proposal Defense.		2 weeks		
Prepare the PPT for the Proposal Defense. Defend the Proposal.		Occurs during committee review		
Schedule and conduct Proposal Defense.		2 weeks		
Revise the Proposal in accordance with Committee Directives.		2 to 4 weeks		This depends on the revisions to the proposal and the overall number of revision iterations .
Create and submit application to the IRB.		1 week		Revisions and approval of Proposal by Committee.
Revise IRB application in accordance with IRB feedback.		2 to 4 weeks		This process may require multiple iterations.

IRB approval to begin research.		1 day	
Begin research.		1 day	
Contact research participants as prescribed in the Proposal, Chapter 3.		2 weeks	
Conduct research via survey and/or participant interviews.		3 to 4 weeks	
Analyze results of the research instruments.		4 weeks	
Author Chapter 4		3 weeks		Personal time availability and approval of your chair to move to this chapter.
Author Chapter 5		3 weeks		Personal time availability and approval of your chair to move to this chapter.
Edit Chapters 4 and 5 for approval to defend the Dissertation.		4 weeks	
Send the Dissertation to Chair.		1 day	
Chair's Review of Dissertation.		2 weeks	
Send the Dissertation to Committee with Chair's approval.		1 day	
Committee Review prior to Final Defense		2 weeks	

Prepare the PPT for the Final Defense.		Occurs during committee review		
Schedule and conduct Final Dissertation Defense.		2 weeks		
Revise the Dissertation in accordance with Committee Directives.		2 to 4 weeks		This depends on the severity of the revisions to the dissertation and the overall number of revision iterations.
Prepare for Library Clearance and Administrative Process for Graduation.		4 weeks		

Creating a project management chart for writing a dissertation involves breaking down the entire process into manageable tasks and organizing them in a logical sequence. Keep in mind that the duration of each task can vary based on your specific requirements and circumstances.

Please note that this is a general template, and you will need to adjust the timeline and tasks based on the specific requirements of your dissertation and your personal working style. Also, dependencies indicate tasks that need to be completed before the next task can start. Customize the chart according to your research plan and any institutional and chair guidelines you need to follow.

DISSERTATION INTENTIONS LOG

<table>
<tr><td>

NAME: _______________________

Time frame for Current Week

ACCOMPLISHMENTS

Accomplishment #1

Accomplishment #2

Accomplishment #3

</td></tr>
<tr><td>

Intentions for Next Week

Intention #1

Intention #2

Intention #3

</td></tr>
<tr><td>

TOTAL PAGES WRITTEN TO DATE:

Chapter 1

Chapter 2

Chapter 3

Chapter 4

Chapter 5

</td></tr>
</table>

TIME SPENT

Goal is for at least 90 minutes per
day Monday _____

Tuesday _____

Wednesday _____

Thursday _____

Friday _____

**YOUR TARGET DATE FOR SENDING
YOUR DISSERTATION PROPOSAL
OR FINAL MANUSCRIPT TO YOUR
CHAIR FOR REVIEW**

QUOTATIONS TO MOTIVATE YOU DURING YOUR DISSERTATION JOURNEY!

These quotes cover various aspects of motivation, perseverance, and success, and they come from a range of inspirational figures throughout history.

1. "You don't have to be great to start, but you have to start to be great." – Zig Ziglar
2. "Believe you can and you're halfway there." – Theodore Roosevelt
3. "Success is not final, failure is not fatal: It is the courage to continue that counts." – Winston Churchill
4. "The only limit to our realization of tomorrow will be our doubts of today." – Franklin D. Roosevelt
5. "You are never too old to set another goal or to dream a new dream." – C.S. Lewis
6. "The only way to do great work is to love what you do." – Steve Jobs
7. "Success is not the key to happiness. Happiness is the key to success. If you love what you are doing, you will be successful." – Albert Schweitzer

8. "In the middle of difficulty lies opportunity." – Albert Einstein
9. "The only person you are destined to become is the person you decide to be." – Ralph Waldo Emerson
10. "Opportunities don't happen, you create them." – Chris Grosser
11. "The future belongs to those who believe in the beauty of their dreams." – Eleanor Roosevelt
12. "Don't watch the clock; do what it does. Keep going." – Sam Levenson
13. "Hardships often prepare ordinary people for an extraordinary destiny." – C.S. Lewis
14. "The journey of a thousand miles begins with one step." – Lao Tzu
15. "Dream big and dare to fail." – Norman Vaughan
16. "The harder you work for something, the greater you'll feel when you achieve it." – Unknown
17. "The only way to achieve the impossible is to believe it is possible." – Charles Kingsleigh (from "Alice in Wonderland" by Lewis Carroll)
18. "It does not matter how slowly you go as long as you do not stop." – Confucius
19. "Believe in yourself and all that you are. Know that there is something inside you that is greater than any obstacle." – Christian D. Larson
20. "Don't be pushed around by the fears in your mind. Be led by the dreams in your heart." – Roy T. Bennett
21. "The only limit to our realization of tomorrow will be our doubts of today." – Franklin D. Roosevelt

22. "If you want to achieve greatness stop asking for permission." – Unknown
23. "What you get by achieving your goals is not as important as what you become by achieving your goals." – Zig Ziglar
24. "Your limitation—it's only your imagination." – Unknown
25. "Push yourself, because no one else is going to do it for you." – Unknown
26. "Great things never come from comfort zones." – Unknown
27. "Dream it. Wish it. Do it." – Unknown
28. "Success doesn't just find you. You have to go out and get it." – Unknown
29. "Dream bigger. Do bigger." – Unknown
30. "Don't stop when you're tired. Stop when you're done." – Unknown
31. "Wake up with determination. Go to bed with satisfaction." – Unknown
32. "Do something today that your future self will thank you for." – Unknown
33. "Little things make big days." – Unknown
34. "It's going to be hard, but hard does not mean impossible." – Unknown
35. "Don't wait for opportunity. Create it." – Unknown
36. "Sometimes we're tested not to show our weaknesses, but to discover our strengths." – Unknown
37. "The key to success is to focus on goals, not obstacles." – Unknown
38. "Your limitation – it's only your imagination." – Unknown
39. "Great things never come from comfort zones." – Unknown

40. "The more control you have over your attention, the more control you have over your future. And it starts with having enough courage to protect your time." – James Clear

41. "It's so easy to say yes. We want to be agreeable, helpful, liked. That's how time disappears and attention becomes fragmented: not in big chunks, but in a thousand small concessions." – James Clear

42. "What you trade your attention for is what your life becomes." – James Clear

RESOURCES TEMPLATE SAMPLE

Author/Title/Year	Topic	Subtopic	Information	Comments	Research Questions / Objectives	Sample	Variables / Instruments	Research Approach	Major Findings / pre telework
Maruyama, Tietzw/From anxiety to assurance: concerns and outcomes of telework/2012	telework	pre and post telework	examines the pre telework expectations of workers with post telework experiences. Prior to teleworking, employees underestimated the possible positive experiences of teleworking and overreacted to possible negative aspects. Overall females found the experience to be better (as it relates to child and home responsibilities) than males in the sales or BD environment (decreased visibility) – overall telework was deemed a positive experience.	possible construct for dissertation					

Maruyama, Tietzw/From anxiety to assurance: concerns and outcomes of telework/2012	telework	motivators	motivators to telework were reduced time and costs for commuting, control and autonomy in work, flexibility, and productivity				
Maruyama, Tietzw/From anxiety to assurance: concerns and outcomes of telework/2012	telework	concerns	lack of interacti+D67on both professional and social; lack of visibility (especially true for females with young children) and professional development, possible loss of motivation; possible increase in home conflicts				
Golden/ Co-workers who telework and the impact on those in the office: Understanding the implications of virtual worker satisfaction and turnover intentions/2007	co-workers of telecommuters	issues	job satisfaction for co-workers is negatively impacted more or less by the amount of time the teleworker is out of the office and face to face time is limited; it is also impacted by the degree of autonomy of the teleworker and the co-worker. The impact can be strong enough for the co-worker to consider leaving the company. This type of arrangement performance flexibility.			autonomy, number of telework days per week, amount of face-to-face interaction	

ABOUT THE AUTHOR

Dr. Ann Gladys has chaired numerous doctoral dissertations. Throughout her work with doctoral candidates, she has witnessed the good, the bad, and the ugly of the dissertation experience! Dr. Gladys has been involved in the dissertation process for more than a decade and has chaired and sat on committees for numerous dissertations. Ann has been a professor in areas that range from Inferential Statistics to Global Leadership and has taught in several doctoral programs (Ph.D., DBA, and Ed.D.).

An author of personal and academic improvement books, Ann's books include;

- *The Invisible Leader,*

- *Mesmerize – How to Give Your Best Presentation Ever,*

- *The Sane Dissertation: Writing Your Dissertation without Losing Your Family, Your Friends, and Your Mind!*

Dr. Gladys is a graduate of the Senior Fellows Program at Harvard, holds a BS in Mathematics from the University of Pittsburgh, and a Master's in Business from Central Michigan University. She received her Doctorate in Organizational Leadership from Pepperdine University where her research focused on leadership in the virtual workspace. Dr. Gladys has presented her research both nationally and internationally. And as the final and most important note, Ann has two grown children, Brett and Kelly, who have given her strength, purpose, and love that surpasses all others.

ENDNOTES

1   National University. (2025). https://www.nu.edu/blog/can-music-help-you-study-and-focus/

2   Miller, H. n.d. Start with Why: A Powerful Way to Lead with Purpose. https://leaders.com/articles/leadership/start-with-why/

3   Sinek, S. n.d. The Golden Circle. https://simonsinek.com/golden-circle/

4   Miller, H. Start with a Why. https://leaders.com/articles/leadership/start-with-why/

5   APA. (2012). Need to Heal Thyself? https://www.apa.org/gradpsych/2012/01/heal

6   UChicago Magazine. (2012, October). *The nature of loneliness*. University of Chicago. https://magazine.uchicago.edu/1012/features/the-nature-of-loneliness.shtml

7   Author(s). (Year). *Title of article. Journal Name, Volume*(Issue), pages. PubMed. https://pubmed.ncbi.nlm.nih.gov/25910392/

8   BBC News. (2024, April 12). New York City to lift vaccine mandate for indoor venues. BBC News. https://www.bbc.com/news/world-us-canada-65461723 3

9   Ibid

10 Roberts, C. M. (2010). The Dissertation Journey. Thousand Oaks, CA: Corwin, a SAGE Company.

11 Ibid

12 Cone, J. D., & Foster, S. L. (2006). *Dissertations and theses from start to finish: Psychology and related fields* (2nd ed).

13 Glatthorn, A. A., & Joyner, R. L. (2005). *Writing the Winning Thesis or Dissertation: A Step-by-Step Guide*. Corwin Press.

14 Roberts, C. M. (2010). The Dissertation Journey. Thousand Oaks, CA: Corwin, a SAGE Company.

15 Creswell, J. W. (2007). Qualitative Inquiry & Research Design. Thousand Oaks, CA: SAGE Publications.

16 Creswell, J. W. (2009, p. 191). Research Design. Thousand Oaks, CA: SAGE Publications.

17 Creswell, J. W. (2013). *Qualitative inquiry and research design: Choosing among five approaches* (3rd ed.). SAGE Publications. https://spada.uns.ac.id/pluginfile.php/510378/mod_resource/content/1/creswell.pdf

18 Ibid.

19 Ibid.

20 LinkedIn. (n.d.). *Tips for maintaining a clean and organized workplace & living space.* https://www.linkedin.com/pulse/tips-maintaining-clean-organized-workplace-living-space-dubai/

21 Washington Post. (2023, June 16). *Avoidance, not anxiety, keeps you stuck.* https://www.washingtonpost.com/wellness/2023/06/16/avoidance-not-anxiety-patterns-strategies/

22 Ibid.

23 Ibid.

24 Ibid.

25 Ibid.

26 Ibid.

27 Ibid.

28 Forbes Advisor. (n.d.). *SMART goals: How to make your goals achievable.* https://www.forbes.com/advisor/business/smart-goals/

29 Thebizsecrets. (n.d.). *Goals* [Facebook post]. Facebook. https://www.facebook.com/thebizsecrets

30 Godin, S. (2023, December). *Leverage.* https://seths.blog/2023/12/leverage/

31 TechTarget. (n.d.). *Pomodoro technique.* https://www.techtarget.com/whatis/definition/pomodoro-technique

32 Tracy, B. (n.d.). *The truth about frogs.* https://www.briantracy.com/blog/time-management/the-truth-about-frogs/

33 Eisenhower. (n.d.). *The Eisenhower Matrix.* https://www.eisenhower.me/eisenhower-matrix/   Clear, J. (n.d.). *The Ivy Lee method.* https://jamesclear.com/ivy-lee

34 Clear, J. (n.d.). *The Ivy Lee method.* https://jamesclear.com/ivy-lee

35 Mind Tools. (n.d.). *David Allen's Getting Things Done (GTD) method.* https://www.mindtools.com/akeyw12/david-allen-getting-things-done

36 Kanban Tool. (n.d.). *What is the Kanban method?* https://kanbantool.com/kanban-method https://kanbantool.com/kanban-method

37 eBillity. (n.d.). *Agile methodology in project management: A comprehensive guide.* https://ebillity.com/blog-hub/agile-methodology-in-project-management-a-comprehensive-guide/

38 Todoist. (n.d.). *The two-minute rule.* https://todoist.com/inspiration/two-minute-rule

40 St. Cloud State University. (n.d.). *Time management tips* [PDF]. https://www.stcloudstate.edu/elhe/_files/documents/dissertation/time-management-tips.pdf

41 The Morning Hero. (n.d.). *Homepage.* https://www.themorninghero.com/

42 BetterUp. (n.d.-a). *All-or-nothing thinking: What it is and how to overcome it.* https://www.betterup.com/blog/all-or-nothing-thinking

43 BetterUp. (n.d.-b). *Where did "perfect is the enemy of good" come from?* https://www.betterup.com/blog/perfect-is-the-enemy-of-good

44 BetterUp. (n.d.-c). *How to take risks: A practical guide.* https://www.betterup.com/blog/how-to-take-risks

45 Washington Post. (2023, June 19). *Growth mindset: How to cultivate it for life and work.* https://www.washingtonpost.com/wellness/2023/06/19/growth-mindset/

46 Masic, I., et al. (2008). *Evidence-based medicine and clinical epidemiology: Basics, principles, and usefulness in daily clinical*

practice. Acta Informatica Medica, 16(4), 219-225. https://www.ncbi.nlm.nih.gov/pmc/articles/PMC1838571/

47 Cone, J. D., & Foster, S. L. (2006). *Dissertations and theses from start to finish: Psychology and related fields* (2nd ed.). American Psychological Association.

48 Creswell, J. W., & Creswell, J. D. (2018). *Research design: Qualitative, quantitative, and mixed methods approaches* (5th ed.). SAGE Publications.

49 Glatthorn, A. A., Boschee, F., Whitehead, B. M., & Boschee, B. F. (2019). *Curriculum leadership: Strategies for development and implementation* (5th ed.). SAGE Publications.

50 American Psychological Association. (2020). *Publication manual of the American Psychological Association* (7th ed.). American Psychological Association.

51 Cone, J. D., & Foster, S. L. (2006). *Dissertations and theses from start to finish: Psychology and related fields* (2nd ed.). American Psychological Association.

52 Creswell, J. W., & Creswell, J. D. (2018). *Research design: Qualitative, quantitative, and mixed methods approaches* (5th ed.). SAGE Publications.

53 Glatthorn, A. A., Boschee, F., Whitehead, B. M., & Boschee, B. F. (2019). *Curriculum leadership: Strategies for development and implementation* (5th ed.). SAGE Publications.

54 American Psychological Association. (2020). *Publication manual of the American Psychological Association* (7th ed.). American Psychological Association.

55 Cone, J. D., & Foster, S. L. (2006). *Dissertations and theses from start to finish: Psychology and related fields* (2nd ed.). American Psychological Association.

56 Creswell, J. W., & Creswell, J. D. (2018). *Research design: Qualitative, quantitative, and mixed methods approaches* (5th ed.). SAGE Publications.

57 Glatthorn, A. A., Boschee, F., Whitehead, B. M., & Boschee, B. F. (2019). *Curriculum leadership: Strategies for development and implementation* (5th ed.). SAGE Publications

58 American Psychological Association. (2020). *Publication manual of the American Psychological Association* (7th ed.). American Psychological Association.

59 Cone, J. D., & Foster, S. L. (2006). *Dissertations and theses from start to finish: Psychology and related fields* (2nd ed.). American Psychological Association.

60 Creswell, J. W., & Creswell, J. D. (2018). *Research design: Qualitative, quantitative, and mixed methods approaches* (5th ed.). SAGE Publications

61 Glatthorn, A. A., Boschee, F., Whitehead, B. M., & Boschee, B. F. (2019). *Curriculum*

62 American Psychological Association. (2020). *Publication manual of the American Psychological Association* (7th ed.). American Psychological Association.

63 Cone, J. D., & Foster, S. L. (2006). *Dissertations and theses from start to finish: Psychology and related fields* (2nd ed.). American Psychological Association.

64 Creswell, J. W., & Creswell, J. D. (2018). *Research design: Qualitative, quantitative, and mixed methods approaches* (5th ed.). SAGE Publications

65 Glatthorn, A. A., Boschee, F., Whitehead, B. M., & Boschee, B. F. (2019). *Curriculum leadership: Strategies for development and implementation* (5th ed.). SAGE Publications.

66 American Psychological Association. (2020). *Publication manual of the American Psychological Association* (7th ed.). American Psychological Association.

67 Creswell, J. W., & Creswell, J. D. (2018). *Research design: Qualitative, quantitative, and mixed methods approaches* (5th ed.). SAGE Publications.